THE LAW OF
BRAND
ATTRACTION

22 Inspired Business Owners From The Brand Builders Club Share Their Most Successful Brand Attraction Strategies

www.thelawofbrandattraction.com

The Law Of Brand Attraction 1

First published in May 2020 Wallen & Martin

ISBN 978-1-912774-55-5 (e-book)

Editor: Sammy Blindell, Andrew Priestley

Contributors:
The rights of Bob Doyle (The Secret), Sammy Blindell (Founder of The Brand Builders Club), Joké Hoetmer, Jennifer Louise, Jean Macdonald, Nikie Piper, Joanna Howes, Loubna Zarrou, Lara Lauder, Pete Cohen, Gayle Edwards, Amanda Frolich, Anne Hayes, Wilma van Dartel, Ruth Driscoll, Caroline Purvey, Kerry Bartley, Brigitte Keane, Ellen Loopstra, Martin Ramsden, Alice Law, Carole Fossey, Vicki Ibaugh, Sarah Cox, and Marie Diamond (The Secret) to be identified as contributing authors of this work have been asserted in accordance with Sections 77 and 78 of the Copyright Designs and Patents Act, 1988.

A CIP catalogue record for this book is available from the British Library.

Contents

Foreword by Bob Doyle
Featured Expert In *The Secret*

I built my business on the Internet.

Back in 1998, through the early 2000s, creating an online business was perfect for me – because it was easy. Too easy.

Back then, I could throw together a few e-books and audios, create my OWN mailing list without the need for third parties, write e-mails to my subscribers that actually got opened, read, and acted upon, and money appeared in my bank account.

I barely knew what I was doing, and things were going great.

Until they weren't.

As the Internet evolved, it got harder and harder for people who "hacked together" a business without any real structure or strategy, to survive.

The *email ATM machine* didn't last very long.

SPAM became a problem. People didn't receive email they'd requested... and even if they did, they opened it less and less.

Marketing became far more sophisticated, and people who had created offline expertise in areas of marketing and business were now bringing their expertise online... and those of us who didn't have a good business foundation started to watch our businesses die on the vine as these new folks did everything a whole lot better.

If you're going to run a successful business today, online or offline, you need systems. You need a long-term strategy. You need a lot of things, actually... and learning what those things are and how to implement them can take you years without the proper support and guidance.

This I know from personal experience.

I was recently asked by Sammy Blindell, the founder of this book, to share a *confession* regarding my business journey on her Confessions of a Global Changemaker Show. Perhaps something I wasn't so proud of, and what I learned.

I told her immediately: "I didn't treat my business like a business."

There is no question that in today's environment, and far into the future, the ability to do business online is going to be almost mandatory... and most certainly advantageous to many messengers such as yourself, who want to reach the masses.

There is simply no better infrastructure in place on the planet to share your value with the world than through the Internet. But unlike when I started, it is far from easy to do and the learning curve is steep.

Many mistakes are made that cost you time, money, and energy. Yes, these *mistakes* are a necessary part of learning. But if you're just blindly trying this and that to try to make your business work online, these mistakes are not going to give you the kind of feedback you need to succeed.

The book you're reading right now is going to save you potentially years of time and frustration.

The authors who have contributed to this book have been chosen because of the excellence they have exhibited in their areas of expertise.

When you scan the chapter titles, you will notice that a good many of them are related to mindset.

I have a particular passion around this subject.

Having taught the Law of Attraction for nearly 20 years and featured on The Secret, I've learned that the number one thing that stops people from succeeding with ANY technique is their WIRING.

I'm literally talking about how your brain has developed its neuro-pathways over the years... and how, left unattended, have created your perception of *reality* of *truth*... of what is good or bad... difficult or easy.

This wiring rules us, and unless we become conscious of it, we will all feel at mercy to the changing tides of our reality.

It is this wiring that you are certain to come up against as you build your personal and professional vision.

Our wiring can prevent us from taking action that we know will serve us – and conversely, cause us to take action in ways we know will not move us forward. All because it's *Just how we are.*

This programming took place over the course of your life, mostly unconsciously. If you're going to create great change in your life, you are going to need to be fiercely conscious about how your mind is interpreting the *input* of your reality.

When we build a business, we're basically forced to learn new things, and be put into situations where we are out of our comfort zone.

If we are at the mercy of our wiring, any existing ideas about discomfort with new situations is going to take over and guide our actions. This is where most people stop their journeys... when it starts to get really uncomfortable.

What most people don't realize is that this discomfort is a GIFT. It is the sign that you've grown to your limits and you are ready to experience new growth when you change and expand the wiring of your brain to be more in alignment with a NEW vision of yourself, that is congruent with the professional success you want to obtain. However, when we do not have the information we need to move confidently through these comfort zones, it's all too easy to rationalize quitting when it gets too hard, or when you see evidence of *failure*.

On the other hand, armed with the right information, you can turn those moments of discomfort into your most powerful motivators. When you can reframe what *discomfort* means, you can use it as a catalyst to grow your vision even BIGGER.

Continuing to be in action requires confidence. And confidence comes from having good information... which is what this book exists to provide you with.

This book is packed with solid advice on mindset, along with specific brand and business strategy.

You'll learn exactly what to do with your newly transformed mindset!

In the process, you'll meet an extraordinary collection of authors, many of whom I've met personally, who are absolutely here to serve you with the benefit of their experience, and their whole hearts.

You hold your future in your hands. What you do with it is up to you.

Wishing you great success!

Bob Doyle

Law of Attraction Teacher, Featured Mentor on 'The Secret' and Creator of the Wealth Beyond Reason program.

Message From Sammy Blindell
The Founder Of The Law Of Brand Attraction
Book Series And The Brand Builders Club

"If you're not leading, you're losing out and for every moment your ideal customers are not investing in you, they are losing out too."

Your ideal customers need you in their lives more than ever before. In fact, as I write this I can imagine that the universe has a big YOU shaped hole in it while it waits for you to rightfully step up and claim your place on the throne of your industry.

The world needs a trusted and credible leader like you to step up and shine like the true lighthouse you are, beaming with all the integrity and credibility that you have worked so hard to build. All of those people that desperately need the transformation you sell right now need you to shine brighter than ever before, so they know exactly where and how to find you. Oh and they don't need you when YOU are ready and everything is perfect in YOUR world. They need you right now... perfectly imperfect, warts and all!

With millions of people consciously seeking answers to what is lacking in their health, spirituality, mindset, relationships, work, finances and business over just the last 30 days alone, your ideal customers are quickly becoming confused and nobody buys in a state of confusion. We now live in a world saturated with thousands of so called 'experts' popping up to compete for the same customers, the same eyeballs, the same attention, the same budgets and the same advertising space as you. If each and every day your dream customers are exposed to in excess of 60,000 brands from the moment they wake up to the moment they go to sleep at night, how do you rent a space in their memory that is so ingrained that they just won't let anyone other than you in?

Never before has there been so much competition in a Global playing field, forcing good business owners, like you, to compete in painful price wars that have reduced the value of your products and services down to an all time low.

With today's Freemium model swiftly saturating the world of business, accessing the highest quality content for free has never been easier. Yet if you are one of the many thousands of entrepreneurs who need help with building a brand that truly stands for something, this book and all of the authors you see before you will get you focused on creating a business that's built on integrity and purpose, so that the profit can follow in great abundance.

No longer do I want to see you burning yourself out, selling your time for money and chasing goals that lead to inconsistent cash flow and time away from the people who matter most to you. Believe me, I know the pain of going through that and I never want you to experience the heartache that follows that kind of lifestyle.

Having spent thirteen years in branding and marketing before launching my first UK based business in 2002, I went on to build six more companies in the business growth sector. After 12 years of relentless drive to make millions of pounds, dollars and euros for my clients, I badly burned out, becoming seriously ill through stress and walking away from my £7.8 million business.

I had to find an alternative solution to do what I love, reach more people with less stress, enjoy more time freedom AND get paid well for it – all while making a difference that matters to the right people.

I found what that was and my purpose revealed itself while I was moving along. I just had to start somewhere and maybe that's where you are right now too – in a transition that is going to lead you on your path to your true purpose. I now have two Global businesses with many thousands of members across my different products. I have created over 1000 mini-courses and have worked with our members to launch theirs too. I run all of this with ZERO employees from the beautiful boat that my husband and I travel around in full time with our four dogs and two cats! If you want your business to make an income through the impact you make, like I do, you will find some brilliant strategies in this book that will help you to get on purpose and create excellent profit right alongside it.

Each of the authors you are about to learn from are genuine human beings that I am proud and honoured to call my friends. I know each and every one of them personally like family, having supported them to build, brand and expand their businesses to a Global audience. They would not be in front of you here if I didn't trust them implicitly and I encourage you to fully embrace the learning they are about to share with you. The lessons they are going to give you cost them greatly to learn, and they have bravely stepped forward and vulnerably shared with you how you can navigate your way safely through the world of brand building without having to learn the hard way, like they did.

Thousands of entrepreneurs are going out of business everyday because there is only so long you can chase money without integrity driven intention behind it. Too many business owners are suffering from unnecessary stress, financial ruin and damaged reputations because they simply don't have the right strategies, systems and plan in place to grow their business profitably and sustainably.

As a result, they are becoming increasingly overwhelmed, burned out, jaded, distracted and making poor critical decisions in a state of stress that is literally killing the business and them along with it.

Please don't let this be you. I believe that it really doesn't have to be this way and that together we can be a force for good that not only raises the quality and value of our products and services, but also the vibration of our services and our value right alongside it.

Ryunosuke Satoro famously said: "Individually, we are one drop. Together, we are an ocean."

So, let's be that One Drop together and deliver an ocean of incredible service that creates a ripple effect bigger than no other that came before us.

I believe in you, so let's do this.

With love,

Sammy xx

PS: Royalties from *The Law of Brand Attraction* go to *Clear Sky Childrens Charity UK.* Clear Sky provides play therapy for vulnerable children aged 4-12 that have witnessed or experienced a trauma. Visit Clear sky at:

www.clear-sky.org

Donate directly at:

https://www.justgiving.com/clearsky

Sammy Blindell - The Brand Builder

Sammy is a multi-award winning international speaker, seven times best selling author and CVO behind How To Build A Brand, The Brand Builders Club and One Drop Movement.

Having spent 13 years in branding and marketing before launching her first business in 2002, Sammy built six more companies in the business growth sector. She launched *www.howtobuildabrand.org* in 2014, taking it from £0 to £18,000 of monthly revenue in 12 weeks with her first book and online program. In February 2017 she launched Brand Builders Club, which has hundreds of members Internationally. Finally, her Global movement, 'One Drop' was founded in April 2019 to celebrate the ripple that is created when Changemakers collaborate rather than compete.

Sammy has created 72 online products and 1000+ online courses to show others how to accomplish in just a few months what it takes most business owners a lifetime to achieve.

Now it's your turn!

www.BrandBuilders.club/Membership

https://www.facebook.com/groups/BrandBuildersClub

https://www.linkedin.com/in/sammyblindellthebrandbuilder

How To Put Your Inner Resilience Into Overdrive!

Joké Hoetmer - The Higher Purpose Pathfinder

"There is a Reason for every Season. Embrace this Season as YOUR Season as no season is ever without reason."

I'm sitting in a boardroom with 12 upright uncomfortable chairs and a table far too big for the room. I notice the dim neon lighting flicker lightly while I feel increasingly intimidated. I'm sitting opposite the solicitor and the buyers, all of whom look like undertakers in their solemn black suits and stern faces, shuffling through their mountains of paperwork. The tension is rising in the room as I wait alone, with my little black briefcase propped up in my lap. I smile nervously to try and mask the feeling of being completely out of my league. My husband, who is also my business partner, is absent and it is very surreal to everyone present, leaving me to singlehandedly represent our side of the sale of the family business.

Suddenly, a prompting in my spirit stirs up the boldness to take them head on, challenging specific points of the contract that have been omitted. Their shocked reaction causes a shift in the atmosphere and a muttering to each other, which results in the Solicitor excusing himself from the room in order to rectify (yes rectify!) the contract in my favour.

'Can you believe their cheek?' I think to myself with a sigh of relief, feeling much less intimidated and more in control for a brief moment. This deal was almost done and over, with only the formality of signing the contract remaining. The feeling of accomplishment swept over me as I sat up, ready to sign the paperwork.

Wait, I don't have to sign anything?

Like a punch in the stomach the news hits me. I nearly fall off my chair in shock as they inform me that only my husband has signing power since he is the sole owner of the company. He has gone behind my back and changed ownership of the company without my knowledge, tricking me into putting the deal together, doing the negotiating, and stressing all the while working and believing that I am an equal partner in the business. It dawns on me that I will never get my share of the money and that he has just sold our business and gone on a safari with my share of everything.

Driving home my head is spinning still in disbelief, I call our family friend Brian. He is such a gentle giant, always filled with love and a kind word, knowing he will cheer me up and give me sound advice.

"Brian, I am leaving Botswana and going to live with my children in South Africa", I blurt out.

There is a long silence and when he speaks, his voice sounds very different.

"Brian what's wrong?" I ask in concern, I can barely hear him through his tears. I take the focus off myself for a brief moment as he asks:

"Joke, do you know where your husband is?" "Yes, he is on a safari doing his thing", I say confidently.

"No Joke, he isn't." He pauses and takes a deep breath... "He is with my wife."

He pauses in his sniffles... "and has been with her for the last five weeks. It's been going on for over a year."

You can hear a pin drop. I have no words, the roller coaster of mixed emotions flood over me. I can't take this all in. So many unanswered questions making my head spin. The betrayal, the lies. How did I not see this? The man I love and trust is having an affair with my best friend right under my nose. I am torn between my own sorrow and my compassion for Brian in his brokenness.

In one short morning, my world falls apart. Suddenly nothing is the same. What started off as an exciting business deal has now turned into my biggest nightmare.

"Be willing to rest in your incubator and grow
to become an innovator."

Joke Hoetmer

"I know I want a house with five bedrooms, close to the schools, a loft room and a view would be a bonus", I confidently say as I am driving with the Estate Agent to view a property in sunny South Africa. She smiles at me and I smile back hoping that she doesn't ask questions and find out that I don't have the money. I quickly add, "I'd love to have a repossessed house that's a fixer upper", as I launch into a conversation about my love for renovating homes in an attempt to distract her.

Within a few days, she finds the one and I sign the letter of intent to purchase, knowing that I really have to play for time; time to find the money somehow. That same evening I go back to the house to take down the *For Sale* board, mentally proclaiming that the house is mine already. I give the security guard instruction to clean up the garden and buy him cigarettes and a Coke, which seems to get him going.

This house is sold. It's mine. Now I just need to pay for it. With my instinct for survival peaked and my inner resilience in overdrive, I start working on a plan to create the future my children and I deserve.

One by one, every step on the plan falls into place. I take bold steps towards the purchase of the house. The agent calls with the good news of my offer acceptance. "I know, I've already sent my furniture truck to that address", I reply. "I trusted and took action." She is shocked and surprised by my bold faith.

Over the next few weeks I get resourceful with the property deals I shared with my now estranged husband. I take careful stock of what is on hand and what is available to explore and monetise. First the deposit is paid, then the transfer fees and again, I carefully consider my resources, my resourcefulness, my negotiation skills and my experience. Each of us has an arsenal of skills and experiences we can draw from if we stopped panicking and carefully considered what they are. As more plans fall into place my confidence grows and my steps get bolder. My faith and trust grows and as a result I accomplish more.

Using an advance from the bank, I commission the build of a flat with a garage next to the house, which I quickly rent out. The rental income pays for the bond in total while my children and I live in the house. I still smile when I think of all the wonderful memories we shared in that home over the years. We lived in the house though their schooling, university, marriages and even my very first grandchild. I realise things could have looked quite different had I not reached deep into my inner resolve, strength and resilience during one of the biggest tests of my lifetime.

The biggest lessons I learned though the various crises I faced in my life have all been greatly character building. They have taught me to be patient, to be kind and to be more tolerant to others including myself.

1. I've learned to make peace with myself through self-forgiveness and the removal of blame and shame, which is by the way one of the hardest things to do.

2. I also believe in forgiving others directly or indirectly.

3. Finding contentment when I am uncomfortable or feel out of control.

4. Coming to terms with the situation as quickly as possible by allowing myself to feel the pain, loss or fear, deciding to let it go and move on.

5. Finding the courage and determination to get out of bed in the morning, wash my face and to say to myself, "I can do this, today is going to be a good day."

6. Finding someone to be accountable to and taking baby steps towards recovery, through constantly encouraging yourself and humouring yourself – laughter is the best medicine - I find my children and grandchildren really help in that regard.

7. Reaching out to others that you respect for advice and allow yourself to be teachable in every possible facet of your life. It helps you to see more clearly.

8. Never compare yourself to others and their journey, rather respect those you admire, be inspired by and learn from them.

9. Only follow people that inspire you and allow them to push your personal boundaries.

10. Stay true to yourself.

Every obstacle, every disaster, every failed business transaction since that day, I've met with the same resilience and resolve. It is always there for us to access and drink from. It's a fountain that never stops flowing. In fact, it flows stronger and stronger the more we drink from it.

I've heard many people refer to resilience as a bounce back muscle. The more adversity we face and overcome, the quicker and faster our bounce back is and the higher we bounce when we get back up.

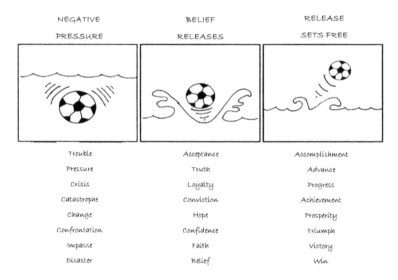

NEGATIVE	BELIEF	RELEASE
PRESSURE	RELEASES	SETS FREE

Trouble	Acceptance	Accomplishment
Pressure	Truth	Advance
Crisis	Loyalty	Progress
Catastrophe	Conviction	Achievement
Change	Hope	Prosperity
Confrontation	Confidence	Triumph
Impasse	Faith	Victory
Disaster	Belief	Win

Never be afraid to fall, to fail and to get back up again. After all, there is a reason for every Season, so embrace this Season as YOUR Season, as no season is ever without reason!

Joké Hoetmer - The Higher Purpose Pathfinder

Joké Hoetmer is a seasoned and intuitive business visionary, public speaker and higher purpose pathfinder, who uses her wealth of real-life and business experience to support and mentor entrepreneurs and their families to navigate and overcome adversity, trauma, loss and pain.

Having successfully founded and established five successful companies in her business career and experienced firsthand the life altering process of entrepreneurship and the resourcefulness required, Joké uses her experience and skills to powerfully facilitate the shift of negative programming and inner transformation for global changemakers. She masterfully impacts and influences through community building and accountability, providing tools and strategies to grow your life and business.

On her *Raw & Real Conversations* podcast, she shares her personal life stories, adventures and unusual experiences with the world, inspiring and motivating others on their path to healing and wholeness. She brings to you an open mind, an open heart and the commitment to support you on your journey.

Facebook.com/Joke.Hoetmer1

Instagram.com/Joke_Hoetmer

Website: Braveandbright.me

Email: info.braveandbright@gmail.com

Success Is In The Numbers -
How You Show Up Is How You Rise Up

Jennifer Louise - The Successful Salon Mentor

"The key to client attraction is to find your Sue."

As I sat in my car with tears flowing down my face, I was fuming. I was more than fuming; I was raging, seething even. I opened the window for some fresh air and the smell of freshly cut grass danced across me, calming me just long enough to open up my phone to look at my Instagram followers and confirm I was in fact UNDATABLE. "Well, that's it then", I said to myself. At 38, two kids, divorced, single for two years and ONLY 1,580 followers. The chance of a happy ever after was shattered after overhearing a conversation between two guys in the gym who were basing if they were or weren't prepared to date a girl on her lack or abundance of Instagram followers! I threw my phone across the car. *"What did they bloody know anyway!"*

I dried my eyes and raced home. Still sat in the car outside my house I checked the salon Instagram account. OMG I may be undatable, but my salon wasn't. It had 5,806 followers! My brain went into an excited frenzy as I realised those guys were right, but in a good way! They were making a decision about how datable people were, based on how many followers they had. So, if they were thinking that way, then maybe my future clients were too. The more I thought about it, I put two and

25

two together and realised that as my salon followers had increased on Instagram, so had my salon bank account. The more people I was attracting to follow my salon, the more popular it was becoming.

This was it. This was Obsessions Salon's time to shine.

Up until that moment I hadn't realised the power of Instagram and content marketing. I had heard numerous times that we must date our customers first if we wanted them to marry into our brand, but I hadn't consciously committed much time or attention to it. The account had grown naturally with me pushing my clients from Facebook to Instagram, but if I was going to do this properly then I had to seriously commit. I made a decision there and then to be 'Instagram famous' as a brand. I wanted to be the best in my area so the numbers meant everything.

I organised an agency to take over the growth of the Obsessions Salon Instagram account and the numbers started to grow. Then to my surprise they went down, then back up again and I was on the edge every day wondering each morning if we had gained or lost followers? This was quickly becoming my next obsession. When I looked at the quality of followers this agency was getting me, I was lost for words. Fake accounts, or accounts in India or Beijing! I mean, my team are great at cutting hair, but no one is going to travel from India for a haircut! I knew there had to be a way to make it work locally, I just hadn't figured it out yet. But one thing I knew for sure was that the social media agency and I were finished.

I got focused on how I could do it myself and found that there are over 500+ million daily active users on Instagram that spend on average 53 minutes a day on the site. Instagram helps 80% of its users to decide whether to buy a product or service and 71% of the world's businesses are on that site. That's a lot of competition. I needed to figure this thing out. I just kept hearing the words over and over in my head, "Jennifer if you delay this journey just another six months, that's six months of growth that your competition are going to have on you. Good luck catching that up again". When I'd overheard those guys in conversation earlier that day, 'She must be okay if she has 3,500 followers', I had become really angry at first. "What an idiot. Is this how we date now?"

But then when I really thought about it, they had done me a BIG favour and changed my way of thinking forever.

Sat around the dinner table that evening with my kids, I was still dancing with the two emotions of anger towards the gym lads and excitement at the salons number count.

"Sam, do you use Instagram to check a girl out before you go on a date with her?" I said to my Son.

"Yeah why?" he said.

"Never mind" left my lips before I became super curious about it. "Why do you?" I asked inquisitively.

"It helps me to see what she likes to do with her spare time, where she works, who she hangs out with... that kind of thing. It helps me to feel like I already know her before we meet.

"Hmmm that makes a lot of sense", I thought.

"Mum listen", said Ellie the 12-year-old marketing brain in our family. "We don't need a phone anymore, we just need Instagram. Look at my phone book".

As she opened it up, I could see the names of only three numbers. Mumzy, Dad, Bro... I couldn't believe what my eyes were seeing only three contacts. But how? She is on that phone 24/7. She has hundreds of friends from all over the seven schools in our local area.

"Mum we make friends on Instagram, then we just follow each other, chat, build a friendship and call each other from within the app".

When I thought about it, I realised that Ellie had done the same thing a few months earlier when she wanted to get her nails done. She had found a picture of the nails she wanted on Instagram, messaged the local salon who had posted the picture and quickly booked with that salon on Instagram. The next time she wanted her nails done, she again looked for a picture of the nails she wanted and booked with that salon right there and then on Instagram.

My ears were ringing loudly as my two children had unlocked the secret to Instagram marketing right there at our dinner table! As I jotted down what they had said, the excitement encapsulated me.

1. Get clients to feel like they know you before they meet you.

2. Make friends, chat, get to know each other, build a relationship and connect with them on Instagram.

3. Showcase all that you do. If a potential client can't see something they are looking for on your page, they will go elsewhere.

Luckily, I already knew my ideal client inside out as I had spent 12 weeks straight studying her after I realised how important it was to know our customers. I pretty much got to know her better than she knew herself. I knew where she lived, what colour her décor was, what car she drove, where she shopped, where she went for coffee with friends, where she went for wine with friends, what her hobbies were, where she ate at the weekend with her husband and where she ate during the week with girlfriends. I then studied the places she loved to go, to find out what they were doing that she was connecting with there. I wanted every post that went out to make her feel that I was talking straight to her.

Her name is *Sue* and she is the most important asset in my business. Even the way we serve the coffee at Obsessions Salon is for *Sue*. The way my team dress is for *Sue*. The salon is decorated for *Sue* and I have woven little parts of all the places she loves into the salon so that it connects with her on a deeper level. And sure enough, more women just like *Sue* started to join the obsession with us.

A few weeks later I was working with a new client when I asked her how she found us? It turns out that she had driven and hour and a half to get a haircut with me because of a post she saw on Instagram. My Instagram post had spoken directly to her. The next new client that came through the door was asked the same question, only to hear a similar response. Then another and another! I had finally figured out how to connect in person AND on social media with our ideal clients.

I'm now driving quality leads to my business in a way that they already feel like they know my team and I before they even walk through our door. I consistently share things that I know for sure will interest them throughout the day. They know what the team are up to, who the team are and I let them experience from beginning to end what it's like inside the salon with us. Our clients get to know the team from afar. I banish their fears of walking into a new salon for the first time... fears of who will be serving them and whether they will like their hair or not. I build connections and friendships through our social media channels by simply connecting with them, managing their fears and expectations in every interaction I have with them.

Every time I post I think, *"How I can serve Sue today?"*

I am focused 100% on my ideal client, not whoever may be watching. Marketing after all, is a disqualification process. It helps potential customers to decide very quickly whether they want to spend their hard-earned money with you or not. If you want to make a massive impact on your customers, don't talk to the masses. *Talk to whoever your version of Sue is.* That's how you get clients off their phones and through your door.

When disaster struck and our High Street was closed down during the Corona Crisis, we were able to pivot quickly. Fortunately, I had heard about the Brand Builders Club just a few weeks before, so I joined and got to work with Sammy and the BBC team straight away on my new strategy... to support millions of other salons around the world to create a successful salon business in the same way I had done. This is how *The Successful Salon Club* was born and in just four weeks we built a new community online of over 900 new prospects. I created my first product and launched *The Successful Salon Owners Podcast,* interviewing some of the biggest celebrities in my industry. Having so many followers on Instagram made it so much easier for me to attract them and it will help you in your business too.

I realised very quickly that Instagram is even better than a website, as it has a heartbeat that your website just doesn't have. It has the same functionalities in marketing as a website, but it enables you to connect straight to the heart of strangers and build a friendship with them; enabling your clients and future clients to feel what you are all about, not just see what you do. It massively strengthens the Google ranking of your website too when connected. I learned about the power of using 'keywords' in my content and posts when I started to learn more about Instagram. I have even taught myself how to build sales funnels inside Instagram to drive business directly into my salon chair on a daily basis and because these clients already love Instagram so much, they share their whole experience with me on... you guessed it, Instagram!

Instagram is literally doing the heavy lifting of my marketing for me. After overhearing that conversation at the gym, my new client percentage grew by 209% and my "local" radius disappeared as clients started traveling from far and wide to come and work with us. This deepened my desire to connect to the right clients even more. I learned all my stylists' ideal clients and I can spot them online a mile off now.

The greatest thing I have learned on this journey is something you can follow immediately. Focus on understanding exactly who your ideal client is and then remove the barriers between your business and them by simply saying hello. Start a conversation with them in a connection way (not a sales way), and your business, like mine, will start to grow everyday one connection at a time. This will give you your perfect loyal ideal client. I haven't spent a thing on Instagram marketing since I sacked that social media agency. I've done it all for free, just one conversation at a time.

So, tell me who your *Sue* is and how you are going to connect with them? After all, you don't just need followers...

How you show up is how you rise up.

Jennifer Louise - The Successful Salon Mentor

Jennifer Louise is an award-winning public speaker, Author, Inspirational change leader, CEO of Obsessions Salon and founder of The Successful Salon Club; a global Academy training salon owners how to get their salons visible, fully booked and celebrating real profit growth with a committed team around them.

Having spent over 16 years as a salon owner and mentor (increasing her NEW client business by over 209%), Jennifer has worked with many salons to develop a strong social media strategy, turning entire teams into mini armies of marketers, pushing their brands further than ever before to get all salon tills ringing.

Jennifer has built two very successful businesses using Instagram strategies to grow her client list. Now she's on a mission to show 10 million salon owners around the world how they can do it too.

https://www.facebook.com/groups/
TheSuccessfulSalonTeamTrainingRoom

https://www.instagram.com/jennifer1ouise

https://www.instagram.com/obsessions.salon

How To Listen To Your Inner Guidance System When It's Time To Get 'On Purpose'

Jean Macdonald - The Midlife Transition Mentor

"There is a plan or path you 'HAVE' to follow and the logic of your purpose may only become clear, as you start moving."

If you are going through, or have been through, a life transition, you will know what a turbulent experience it can be. Whether that transition is making a big shift in the direction of your business, leaving a long-term relationship, or a life change that is taking you on a different path, being ready for that change is not always something we have time to prepare for.

It is not just the physical experience that creates the external shifts that you can physically see around you. There are also emotional and mental shifts that are also going on at the same time, which can leave you feeling overwhelmed, mentally exhausted and even like giving up.

I can promise you though that these feelings are not the beginning of the end, but the end of just one phase of your life and the beginning of your next one. I know this because of my age and my experience of living as both a woman and a man in the same body, along with being in the same relationship for over 40 years.

It is increasingly recognised and acknowledged that when we shift from one chapter of our life to the next, it is a significant transformation. It can be just like the transformation from a child to an adolescent. It's a big deal. And if you are going through a shift in your business right now, this is the best time to take stock of where you have been, where you are now and where you are going.

There was a time when the ground totally shifted for me and I thought the world was going to end. At that time, in 2012, I had been living as a man most of the time, but had developed a second life as a woman over the previous twenty years.

I kept these two lives rigorously separate and a very few people knew my secret. I enjoyed walking from one life into the other and had two groups of friends who only knew me as Jean or John.

Then I was on a spiritual training retreat with about 30 other people and received a strong spiritual message, twice! That was that I had not been given this privilege of living in both genders for my personal pleasure and enjoyment. I was told it was my time to 'go public' and take up my mission. At the time I had no idea what my mission could be.

What I did know was that I was scared stiff. I and the other attendees on the retreat had our own Facebook Group and so I decided as the first step to go public on that. I wrote a Post telling them my secret and then hesitated for about half an hour before pressing the Send button. Needless to say the response from the Group was immensely supportive, but it still was a surprise to me.

It was also the first time I remember using the phrase 'What the hell do you think you are doing?' I now know this is called 'Imposter Syndrome' and I recognised it from earlier in my career.

Years ago, I had left a successful corporate career with a flash company car to start a business with my wife. We shared a clapped out Mini and had two pre-school age children. Looking back, I think we must have been mad. But we survived and then succeeded.

Later on, we embarked on a Network Marketing career, not particularly to make money for ourselves but we felt it could provide a vehicle for other people to break out of their financial constraints. It was a difficult time for the reputation of Network Marketing, in the shadow of the Pyramid schemes, but we stuck at it through the tough early days. Despite incurring the hostility of a lot of people we knew, we managed to help a lot of people change their lives and made a lot of money ourselves.

In both cases, what I learned was that you have to do what that inner impulse is calling you to do. It may seem illogical at the time, but the true value becomes clear later.

Coming back to 2012, I could have relied on those previous lessons, but this was a different league of arrogance; to believe that after living successfully as a man for most of my life I could contribute anything useful to the world masquerading as a woman.

I went underground for a year or two and busied myself in other projects, but the impulse would not go away. Eventually, I started to write a book about love and sex among older people. During the writing of that concept, the Midlife Woman emerged. I didn't invent the term. It came from Marianne Williamson. I had read her book *The Age of Miracles – In praise of the new Midlife Women* some time before. My book was eventually called, *Love Sex and the Midlife Woman*.

I published the book at the end of 2016 with a picture of Jean on the cover and in the 'About the Author biography' section buried at the back of the book. I thought the job was done. But 'the universe' had other ideas!

First my book hit the market with a soundless splash and disappeared under water without trace. It became clear that if I were to have any impact, I would have to do more.

At first this was all about getting attention for the book. One of the things I realised while writing the book had been that most of my friends as Jean in previous years were midlife women.

From them I learned much about their hopes, disappointments, and frustrations... particularly with midlife men. This became a mainstay in writing the book and subsequent articles about intimate love and partnerships in middle life.

Later, it became putting myself out there as an unapologetic advocate for the cause of empowering midlife women. Needless to say the 'Imposter Syndrome' was still screaming *What do you think you are doing?*

Finally, the idea of the New Midlife Woman Community emerged as a vehicle to really help my target market. Sammy took me under her wing in the Brand Builders Club and reassured me that I was in more of an authority position than most to share with Midlife Women what is going on for their Midlife Man, because I am both. I realised that Sammy was right and immediately my imposter syndrome disappeared.

I am encouraged to believe that I am on the right track by wonderful encouragement, support and love from the other Brand Builders in this book.

So what are the lessons you can learn from my journey?

1. There is a plan or path you 'HAVE' to follow and the logic of your purpose may only become clear, as you start moving.

2. You can say it comes from your higher self, the 'Universe' or some form of God. But what I have concluded is that your higher purpose is not imposed on you from above.
   It is something you feel from within and if you don't listen to it things will just continue to feel out of place until you do!

3. The mission, plan and path are known to you and if you are ever in doubt, go deep inside and check.

4. If you ever deviate from your path, you will pretty soon feel it. When others and logic are saying 'stop', ignore anything and anyone other than your own inner guidance system.
   If a time is right to stop you will know it.

5. Some things may happen that are apparently irrelevant to you at the time, but later all will fall into place as part of the 'grand plan'.

You have a destiny to do something significant and if you don't know it yet, you will. If the path seems to be blocked, trust in the power behind you, above you and around you to drive you in the direction you need to go.

Jean Macdonald - The Midlife Transition Mentor

Jean believes Midlife Women can change society when they believe in themselves. However in their transition from being a young woman to a successful midlife woman, they encounter many barriers obstacles and challenges.

Jean has created the New Midlife Woman Community to help women in transition to build a better lifestyle and lovestyle for the second half of their lives.

Jean worked in business and marketing for many years and then founded a multi-million business in the North West of England. Since then she has written many self-development books and run several education enterprises.

Jean has an unusual perspective on intimate relationships and gender because she has lived as a man and woman and can see relationship issues from both the feminine and masculine points of view. She has been in the same relationship for over 40 years.

https://www.facebook.com/newmidlifewoman

https://www.facebook.com/groups/271573019956513

Be Your Own Kind Of Awesome...
Own It And Give Yourself Permission
To Be Everything You Want To Be!

Nikie Piper - The Awesome Life Creator

"Make a difference by being the difference."

It's all about choices. Your growth or expansion is not just determined by everything that is going well in your life, but by what you can learn from the things that are not going so well. The mistakes, the pain, the challenges, and the frustrations. It is important to understand that the setbacks that you 'perceive' are really just learning and growth in disguise.

It's only by taking action, in one form or another, that you can understand what doesn't work, and move closer to what does. No matter what anyone says, you are going to experience challenges of some description in your business whether you like it or not; it's how you respond to and handle those challenges that counts. Re-framing the lesson and taking something away from each situation that is not as you expect, is an art best learned quickly.

As a coach of mine once said, the best time to have started anything is the exact number years ago that *your thing* came into being. The next best time is now! For me that meant I was on the right track and the Universe had given me the perfect time for my lessons. You can't just go back in time to be at the beginning of the rise of 'your thing,' so why not make now the perfect time?

Is now your time to make a difference or are you hiding?

I'm not going to shy away from being who I truly am, and of owning my story. Have I always felt worthy to do the things I've done in my life? No, not in the least, but you know what— I'm owning them anyway.

I hope the little part of my journey I share with you here will help and inspire you, drive you to think about how you react to things that are going on in your business and your life. I will impart some of my knowledge in the best way I know how and possibly, very possibly, save you some pain.

Let's face it, some of my best learning has come about as a result of business experiences I would rather had not happened. I have created, or been a part of, multiple businesses that just didn't seem to work for me or weren't in alignment with me no matter how hard I tried or wanted them to be. In hindsight, I was expecting them to fix something in me, to give me my purpose and glory, not to amplify my shortcomings and woes.

I had been involved in many different businesses, ideas, and ways of making money (all of which seemed perfect at the time). From working by myself as a specialist contractor; being a driving instructor; creating a company partnership – twice; starting a jewellery company that made my own designs; buying volume stock that left me decidedly in debt; running a consultancy for technology funding programs; to getting into a handful of different network marketing companies that didn't work for me, and finding the one that does.

All these experiences have added up, making me who I am. I've learned from everything that I have done, learned what makes me tick, what I'm passionate about, what I like doing and what I don't. I've learned the types of people with whom I wish to work with both as clients and partners. Most importantly I've learned that it's not what happens to you, but how you handle it and your thought processes that count. They count beyond measure.

What people don't tell you about life, business or the way we *see* our existence, is that you are the only one who creates your reality: it's not the outside that needs fixing, the external situations and challenges are not generally the problem, as I discovered. Looking for external answers to everything that is going on inside is a behaviour that many of us have - myself included until recently.

The key to understand and accept, as the Law of Attraction states, is everything that you have and that is in your life, is something that you have created in one form or another. That was a bitter pill for me to swallow, and once realisation dawned it took some processing and some ownership.

So be your own kind of *all of them*, the experiences, the learning and the outcomes. YOU are that golden thread that runs through everything you do: the thread that's going to shine through in absolutely everything you own and create. It's that which will then tie back into everything you're doing and how you do it.

Nobody ever starts a business with the conscious intention that it should fail, with the intention of it not doing, and being, exactly what they want it to do. And the truth is, many businesses do fail. Many businesses don't reach the expectations of the people that started them, mine included.

It's your inner passion and inner resonance with what you're doing that's key. It's got to be the very core being of you, not a *thing* because you want it to be, or you think it'll be a good choice!

In 2017, I attended my first ever major personal development event and it changed my life. Things started to happen and to change for me because my thinking had been changed.

I started doing things differently and I finally understood the meaning of *if you want things to change, you have change!*

Shortly after that event, in a fit of frustration with my current life, I wrote out everything I wanted my business to be about. I didn't know what I wanted to do exactly, but I did have a vision of how I wanted to be and to feel, and what types of things I wanted to have in my business. So, I wrote it out. It was a labour of love that just spilled out on to the pages. That writing took the form of a website that I never published. I wrote out every aspect of what I wanted to do within those pages.

A few years later it's unfolding in ways I could never have imagined or designed myself or even have dreamt of. When I re-discovered that website, left unloved and untouched with the service provider, I was astounded. Honestly, I know it's a bit 'Tony Robbins,' but I had literally created my date with destiny! I had allowed my mind to create the life I wanted away from depression and debt, and it blew me away.

Realisation dawned: your thoughts are powerful. I had set my intention and subconsciously I was working my way towards what I wanted. Because it resonated with me, because it's so core to what I believe and how I am, and what I truly want to do.

The biggest learning for me over the years is to keep a consistent *be-ing* with myself, with those that I know and the rest of the world.

It's how YOU show up, how you are and what you do.

It's the words you speak and write.

It's the actions you take both inside and out.

It's about doing what you said you were going to do, even though the enthusiasm to do it has long gone.

It's about self-love; loving you enough to own your words, your actions, and your intentions.

It's being there, especially to and for yourself. After all, you can only come from a place of your own truth.

It's thinking, intending and creating your own reality. And about giving yourself permission to do just that. Because if you don't know how to give yourself the love you need, how is anybody else going to?

It's a journey, as the whole of your life is. It's how you walk that journey that counts. And if you're true to you, the world is true with you. These principles are now what I stand by and for, both for me as a person and in my businesses.

The way it works, as I see it, is the ability to be consistently open and the willingness to look at the world in different ways. The way you think can be learned and, as the saying goes, if you can change your thinking, then you can change your life.

Recognize the power of intention, the immense power of writing things down. The key to that kingdom you are looking for is within - perhaps you simply haven't experienced that yet. So, embrace your challenges and the things that are not working for you, for they are only not working at one level. Perhaps they are working perfectly in ways that you can't see right now?

Cover these experiences with gratitude and love and ask yourself *How do I reframe these into learning and lessons that I can take forward?* I would ask you *How do you know things weren't supposed to turn out this way in order for you to take the path you were really intended to be on?*

Finally, I have learned that you need to let go of everything inside that you 'think' you should be, of 'how' others think you should be, and of how you 'believe' you are seen.

Let it go and be free.

Your experiences shape you to who you are. Be sure not to let anyone else's judgement of you change that.

Who you are is your gift – your own kind of awesome.

Nikie Piper - The Awesome Life Creator

Nikie has first-hand experience at creating her life with her thoughts and the power of intention. Rising from the depths of depression, twice being made redundant from a job she loved and separating from her husband of 24 years. It took all her positive thinking, mental fitness and positive action to climb out of £60,000 worth of outstanding debt and to rise from earning less than £400 a month and relying on friends to support her.

Throughout this time Nikie started to journal and born out of frustration with not being able to find anything on the market that fulfilled her journaling needs, Nikie created her own range using her stunning gift in photography. Nikie is the owner and founder of My Awesome Life Ltd, through which she now guides, teaches, and supports others in changing their 'traditional' thinking habits through proven journaling processes, online programs, live events and books.

www.myawesomelife.co.uk

www.facebook.com/MyAwesomeLifeLtd

Unlock Your Mind, Unlock Your Impact... Be In Charge Of Your Results

Joanna Howes - The Change Creator

"Why go out of your mind when you can unlock its power instead?"

I thought I had finally made it. Seated in Business Class, champagne in hand, on a flight I didn't have to pay for. I'd had worse days!

I'd just turned 39, and had been offered my dream job in Australia at the world's most awarded agency, to join their Executive team. This is what I had spent the past 20 years working relentlessly towards. I had finally completed my life's purpose of making my Dad proud. His image was firm in my mind as we cruised above the clouds.

Yet within 8 months of arriving Down Under my world was turned upside down and started to collapse around me. I had a big choice to make - be a victim and blame the world or dig deep within me and take charge. Ultimately, it was this decision that changed the course of my life in ways I could never have previously fathomed and equipped me with tools that I'm going to share with you so you can begin your journey. But first, the story that led to this point of radical change.

My drive and determination to succeed started when 18 years

old. I walked into my front room to find Dad sitting on the couch resting on his arm. Mum had mentioned he wasn't feeling well, so I approached cautiously and asked if he was okay. He looked at me and within a second he was gone! I called out to my Mum and brother and I did everything I could think of to save his life.

That same night my Nan had a heart attack and my poor Grandad had an inconceivable choice to make: to be with his wife or his daughter. In those few hours all of our lives had dramatically changed. In truth, this was the start of six years of further traumatic events. I look back and recognize that night as being the moment when a switch flicked within me. I changed from the shy, quiet girl who hid from the world, to having the overdriving need to prove that I could succeed no matter what. To keep Dad alive in my mind, I needed to achieve success. I had to get to the top so he could be proud of me.

This gave me strength in the years that followed as I focused my mind on this new goal. I worked all the hours I could and made sure that I took every single opportunity that came my way. I stayed late, I worked weekends, I hit targets, I tended to be 'the last one standing'. As long as I was 'doing well' and 'succeeding' I was worthy. I needed to feel like I was achieving something to counteract the feelings of failure when I remembered that vivid night in our front room.

The night I 'failed' to save my Dad's life.

So, to be telling my friends and family I was off to join the Executive team in a top agency in Australia, was one of my proudest moments (albeit the hardest - having to leave them behind). But now, I would be able to be 40 years old and say, 'I'd made it!'.

How wrong could I have been.

Very quickly I knew it wasn't going to work. The job had been mis-sold to me, the expectations of my role were different to what had been set out and it was very obvious that some of the team just didn't want me there. I found myself in a dog-eat-dog culture and experienced for the first time a culture that thrived off passive aggressive treatment. My mind couldn't cope. Being so far from home, I started to doubt myself, completely losing any sense of who I was and crippled with anxiety. On top of all this I felt silenced. I was embarrassed to fail, to tell people that my exciting 'dream job' didn't work out, and that I would be coming home. So, I said nothing, and instead found my mind unravelling before me and all sense of purpose quickly disappearing.

One evening, while scrolling mindlessly on Facebook, an ad for The Coaching Institute appeared with an offer to attend their weekend foundations training. I had been interested in coaching before I left the UK and, with nothing left to lose, I thought: 'Let's see what this is all about.'

I remember walking in that chilly Friday morning, so apprehensive, feeling the self-doubt that had now become second-nature creeping in. I persevered, I took my seat towards the back and I listened to what was about to be the most transformational two days of my life. Without knowing it, I was being given the tools to learn how to unlock my mind. I started to make sense of why I felt the need to prove myself and began to understand how I can now create the impact I wanted for me, for the next 40 years. The release of the pain in my chest, from the realisation that I was in charge of my results left me feeling empowered and set free to learn and become who I wanted to be.

Fast forward to today, and after leaving Australia with my head held high two years ago, I am now running my own business, supporting leaders to access their inner power and unlock their full potential. I can say with certainty that I haven't looked back. Yes, many times it is hard to be an entrepreneur; the overwhelming frustration of not knowing how to do everything leads to moments of despair. But now I have the keys to my mind. I can choose how I respond to what comes my way, be it good or bad. I've learned to ask for help. I've realised that I didn't need to be the superhero anymore.

In fact, if there's only one takeaway I can give to you, it is to invest in you.

The lessons I've learned with my experiences are priceless. Here are some key learnings I'd love to share with you that you can apply to your own journey.

1. You are not your mind – Your mind is a tool for you to use and guide to achieve what you want. Like a Sat Nav, you programme the destination and off you go. Okay, like a Sat Nav it can go off track at times, but I'll cover what to do then in the next tip.

2. What you focus on is what you get – Focusing on opportunities and possibilities will create a magnetic attraction to you in potential customers. Focus on the opposite and that is also what you will get, so keep focused on what you DO want to attract.

3. You are fully responsible for all your choices and actions – Right! No more blaming others, no judging and no more 'victim' behaviour. You are in control of how you choose to respond, regardless of the situation or event.

4. Repetition opens opportunities – Your mind has been working the same way for a long time. Autopilot as such. You need to guide it to change and build new neuro networks. This can only be done through repetition. Read the same book three times, watch the video again and again. After doing this for a period of time you will wake up one morning and it will just click.

5. Upgrade your personal standards – Put personal standards in place. Eg: complete what you commit to do, always give 100 per cent. Learn from the people who have already achieved the success you want and model their standards. That is why I joined the Brand Builders Club. Upgrading your standards and continuing to rise and meet them informs your mind that you can keep promises to yourself. So, 'show up' for yourself and start operating at a new level of impact.

6. Reset your beliefs about you – Beliefs are not real. They are what

we have either been conditioned to believe about ourselves, or ones we have chosen to believe. Identifying the beliefs that could be holding you back is essential to unlocking your mind. If you believe you are not the smartest in the room, you never will be as your brain will always hunt for evidence to support this belief. However, you do have the power to change your limiting beliefs as you created them in them first place!

It's now over to you. Are you ready to unlock your mind and access the power you have within you to accelerate your impact and results? I hope you choose to; I truly believe we are all capable of living the life we dream and, let me tell you, it's sometimes a lot closer than you think.

Now, as I raise my glass of champagne to you and your success - this time very much on firm ground - I know with every fibre of my being that Dad is proud of me.

Joanna Howes - The Change Creator

Joanna Howes is a leading international change creator, coach and speaker. She's the founder of a global mentoring programme for leaders and business owners to access their inner power, bring out the best in themselves and others and lead the way in creating our new global economy.

Joanna spent 19 years working internationally in some of the most awarded advertising agencies in the world, innovating their business operations and leading their multi-disciplined teams to success. In 2016 she became a professional coach and accredited behavioural profiler after training at the No 1 coaching school in Australia.

Joanna's mission is to show others how they too can unlock their full potential, create impact and achieve ultimate success while staying true to themselves.

www.joannahowes.com

www.facebook.com/thechangecreators

The A.C.T.I.O.N. Equation...
How To Be A Strategic Dynamo
In Your Business

Loubna Zarrou - The ACTION Accelerator

*"Whatever you do, have fun doing it.
It will make a huge difference."*

Have you ever heard that to be successful you must work hard? Give it a 1000%. Even nowadays you will find people talking about hustling, slaying, grinding, and crushing your way to success. There is a notion in society that to be successful we have got to literally take ourselves to the point of burnout. Here is an example of how this plays out ... You call a friend and ask: "How are you?" The first thing they say is: "I am busy". Doing activity after activity is apparently the norm for many. On the other hand, I have spoken to many Corporate Professionals and Entrepreneurs who tell me that despite working hard, they are not happy, nor do they feel fulfilled. Fulfilment comes from achieving something you desire aka achieving your goals. When I dig deeper, they tell me there is a lot in their lives that requires their attention. Career, a business, health, relationships, and the list goes on. The route to achievement in this model is hard work. The negative impact of this, you can see in the numbers on high levels of stress and burnout.

Unfortunately, this message was ingrained in me very early in life. "Work hard if you want to be successful," he said, "and give it 200%."

I know my Father had no idea of the impact these words would have on me, as he loves me and wants the best for me. Yet, I took his words to heart and worked hard for an exceedingly long time. As an immigrant in a different country with a whole different culture, I knew, I was going to be perceived and judged as being different. I made up for that difference by working twice as hard at my success.

Imagine being programmed to work twice as hard whilst going through high school, university, and my career as a Project Manager and Change Manager. My belief was that this was the only way. The consequences of this belief were that I spent most of the time at work. I had little time for my friends and family, because there was always something to be working on. Some of my colleagues did not like me much because I was setting a standard in the workplace they did not want to live up to. The rewards were amazing, I got bonuses and promotions in record speed. I also got to deal with jealousy because there were colleagues that were not happy. I was getting these rewards and they were not, especially those that had been working there longer than I had been. Despite working hard, some goals were impossible to achieve, which left me frustrated. I used that frustration as fuel to work even harder, because remember my conditioning!

Until one day, that belief was shattered by an impactful event. I was working as an IT-Auditor with an amazing Deputy Director. We had the same passion, enthusiasm, and work ethic - working together was a treat. Weeks before, I had overheard the Deputy Director and Manager talking to some of my colleagues in another room. They were talking about a request from a client for something innovative. Something they had never done before! Immediately, I thought this was my chance to become successful on something completely new. So, I jumped out of my chair, walked into the other room, and said: I want to do this project! My colleagues looked at me with fire in their eyes. Apparently, they had been trying to convince management to say no to the client because it was too innovative, and they were not prepared for it. They saw risks where I saw opportunity. Needless to say, the project was a go and straight away the Deputy Director and I got to work on doing this project and creating this innovative report. Despite the late nights, I still remember feeling amazing. The client was incredibly happy, I learned later, and this was the start of a new product that many clients in the following years were happy we could offer. Then came the defining moment. The Director called us all into the living room area of the office to make an announcement. He announced that the Deputy Director – whom I had so admired - was on indefinite leave as she was burned out! I was shocked and, of course, worried.

In that moment, my first thoughts were, if she can get burned out, so can I. We give the same energy and passion to our work. I got a glimpse into my possible future if I kept doing what I was doing. I vowed I was going to do whatever it takes to avoid that from happening. I decided to reprogram my belief of *You must work hard to be successful.* This belief had served me well but no more. This inspired me to take the journey to discover ways to make work fun yet still successful. The Strategic Dynamo was born. I became the person others admired for acting in a fun and relaxed way. I began speaking about the Science of Happiness and how to avoid the pitfalls of hard work. In this new guise, I realized I was also having a major impact on people in terms of strategy, goal-setting, and goal achievement. I naturally support people to take action to achieve their goals without the risk of burnout.

Now you may be wondering what is wrong with hard work – short answer, nothing! The problem is when hard work is translated into 'busyness' instead of a strategy and intentional actions. You can be doing lots of things, but not getting anywhere, which in turn creates a feeling of being unfulfilled. Now if you are like me, you started your business because you want to make an impact, a Global impact. To achieve this, you need to take action!   You might be thinking of course, *Doesn't everyone know this already?* Clearly not, as I have found out over the last 20 years, knowing is not the same as doing. Let us go through a simple process to get you started.

As an Entrepreneur you want to make an impact, that is the goal you want to achieve by a certain point in time. You are further along than those who do not set any goals. However, supposing you have more than one goal? Especially if you are a multi-passionate person like me! To increase the likelihood of achieving your goal, it is important to focus on one goal. I have heard someone say once, you can increase the chance of success by 80% by mono-tasking instead of multi-tasking.

- **Step 1 - Grab a piece of paper and pen and write your goal down.**

- **Step 2 - Think about why this goal is important to you.**
  What will achieving this goal mean to you? Write this down too. I am asking you to do this because it is easy to set a goal and brainstorm about actions you need to take to achieve it. But, if achieving the goal does not matter to you enough, your motivation will die along the way. This will leave you frustrated, which puts you in a downward spiral.

- **Step 3 - Come up with actions that will contribute to achieving your goal.** It is important here to break it down into small steps you can take consistently every day. By doing this you lower the threshold of resistance and avoid procrastination. In coming up with actions, bear in mind, that the actions create small wins for you. This will motivate you even more to keep going. At this moment, I want you to take out your diary or calendar and schedule the execution of the actions right now In doing this right now, you are starting to train your brain in taking action immediately. And have you noticed... this could be your first win!

- **Step 4 - Think about what could hold you back in taking action.** What are some of the roadblocks you will inevitably encounter? One of them is going to be distractions. We live in a world with so many distractions. So, for every roadblock you can come up with, come up with a strategy to deal with it.

- **Step 5 - Reward yourself!** How are you going to reward yourself for taking action? Write this down, so you have something to look forward to.

These are the first steps in becoming a Strategic Dynamo. If we had more time, I would be able to go through it in more depth. For now, you can get started. Right about now, you might have started thinking this is simple, too simple. You would be right, it is simple, but not easy. Remember earlier, we do not always do what we know, and we take the simple things for granted. Most of us are not born with the habit of action taking for it is an art and a deliberate practice. It takes effort to make it effortlessly in the future and I know you can do it.

Have fun!

Loubna Zarrou - The ACTION Accelerator

Loubna Zarrou is an international bestselling author, professional speaker and multi-award-winning Strategic Dynamo who is globally recognized for her extraordinary skill of being able to mentor Entrepreneurs to gain clarity, focus and momentum with lightning speed.

Before starting her business and becoming the CEO of The Exponential Hero, Loubna spent over 18 years managing projects both in IT as well as change management in the corporate sector. It was during these years that Loubna was able to hone and utilize her expertise in helping people enhance their happiness at work, as well as strategies for more success in the boardroom.

Loubna has now been able to take this a step further with her unique and innovative approach to mentoring through her A.C.T.I.O.N. process and regularly speaks to her audience on the importance of strategy, planning and the science of happiness to increase their impact, influence and income.

https://www.linkedin.com/in/loubnazarrou

https://www.facebook.com/loubnazarrouofficial

https://www.exponentialhero.com

Show Up and Shine... Use your Presence, Poise And Pitch To Unlock Your Hidden Confidence

Lara Lauder - The Personal Brand Stylist

"Don't buy business cards - Be your BEST business card.
Investing in yourself is the best investment you will ever make."

"Lara, I'm not going to give you the job."

"Oh," I manage to utter from my mouth, eyes fighting back the prickle of tears as I try to look through him, not at him, in an attempt to hide my disappointment.

"No, I'm not going to give you the job of teaching assistant because I believe you could be the teacher."

This memory is firmly etched in every fibre of my being. I had no idea at the time that the words of this conversation would stay with me, shape me and remind me of how far I have come during the course of my life.

Mr. Waddington, Headmaster of Ryde Junior School, saw something in me that day that no one else had. He saw me, not the façade I was hiding behind, but me. He saw my potential, just bursting to be set free from the leash of life on the Isle of Wight in the late 1980s. In those few moments he gave me a gift that I have treasured and have been able to pass on to others. This gift is the skill of unlocking people's hidden confidence, ensuring they're able to harness their unique skills and talents to shine even brighter.

The word *authentic* is bantered around so much, but how many of us truly show up as who we really are? You might think you do but often it takes a major turn in life, a trauma for us to deeply connect with ourselves and free us from a life that others wanted for us, or we have found ourselves in. Can you honestly say you have reached your full potential? Or are you constantly striving for more, a better way, a better life, a better business?

As experts in our chosen field, we know our businesses better than anyone else. However, your business potential and growth is only as big as your 'self' and your confidence. Are you struggling to attract new clients, clinch the deal and get your message heard? It's worth considering if the help you require to move your business forward is not, for example, investment in a new website, a series of adverts, or a social media course - but an investment in yourself! I'm talking about you investing in the development of your Personal Presence and thereby an investment in YOU!

How many of us as young adults were moulded and shaped by our parents, their experiences and fears? I certainly wasn't empowered to go forth into the world, explore, have a voice and achieve anything I wanted. This is not a criticism of my parents but rather an observation. If you had met me then you would not have suspected any of this. Most would say I oozed confidence, vibrancy and had a way with words that my mum described as being able to 'sell ice to Eskimos'! But inside it was a different story. There was still a default setting of being too trusting, not being able to say 'no' and doing things to please others to my own detriment, happiness and contentment.

There have been pockets of me 'showing up and shining' over the years. A year after getting married, in my second year of teaching, my husband was made redundant. Rather than sitting on my backside waiting for our house to be repossessed, I went into full Lara action mode. I decided to buy a Global Travel

Franchise with the money my grandmother had left me, with the aim of securing greater financial security for myself and my husband. With the confidence I had gained from having stepped out of my comfort zone, to go off and get a 2:1 BEd (Hons) degree and the first teaching job I applied for, I knew that when I truly applied myself I could achieve anything. I just needed to replicate that faith Mr. Waddington had ignited.

How I worked as a full-time teacher by day and as a travel agent by night I will never know! I rapidly built up a client base putting together detailed itineraries. I did this job well, so much so that I soon had to give up teaching.

I was the face of that business and its reputation was me, my voice, my passion and my due diligence. I walked my walk and talked my talk. I didn't own a box of business cards, I didn't need to as I was my best business card. I made sure every client walked away feeling like they were my only VIP. I took time to listen to my clients, to better understand them and discover what was important for them. The end result being, the sale of this thriving franchise just a few years later for four times my initial investment.

Have you noticed that life has a habit of knocking you down though? You can be the bubbliest person in the world, but when someone or something bursts that bubble, the air oozes out and you go horribly flat and so does your confidence. As you deflate, your sparkle and shine becomes dull and starts to rust. For some this bubble will burst because of a breakup, a change of job or career, illness, the loss of a loved one or even just adjusting to being a parent.

My bubble burst big time eight years ago with elements of all the above. At the time, I had gone back to teaching after my marriage break up and had risen through the ranks at school, from entering on a part time 10-week maternity contract to securing a position as an Assistant Headteacher in just four years. This wasn't just Lara action mode, it was Lara supersonic action mode. I realise now, however, it comes with a very big health warning! I still remember sacrificing a doctor's appointment because the Deputy Head guilt tripped me into going to the staff meeting instead. In short, something as small as a bad sore throat turned into an infection of the heart and pericarditis. At the same time, I was also told I had Supraventricular Tachycardia, the effects of which have been long term and still affect me today. Where was my voice then? Was I honouring, respecting and standing up for myself? NO! I lacked the confidence and feeling of self-worth when it mattered the most because I was downtrodden, stressed and overworked. I had lost all perspective of what was really important.

So how have I made sure that never happens again?

I have developed my own unique secret weapon. It's called *My Cloak of Confidence* and is the icing on the cake in terms of Personal Brand Strategy. It focusses on YOU, so you can succeed and experience personal and business growth by being truly you; authentic by being *Your Best Business Card*. A key component of this is something I experienced personally four years ago whilst still dealing with ill health. At the time I was not working, feeling on the scrap heap, full of ideas though, wanting more for myself, wanting my Lara sparkle back but knowing I needed to adopt a good home/work life balance. I discovered through Colour Analysis, the shades of colour that naturally complimented my skin tone, made my eyes shine bright and made me look well. I could not believe that something so simple as colour could have such a massively positive effect on my health and wellbeing. It was life changing!

When you combine this colour knowledge with understanding and accepting your unique body shape and personality, something magical happens. All those insecurities about body shape start to fade away; the inner voice that chips away at you, making you question *Do I look ok, Does this suit me? What will others think of me?* are replaced with an inner smile, a light that shines so brightly on the inside that it radiates on the outside.

I experienced a reconnection with myself, an understanding and an acceptance. I found me again and with my confidence starting to return, the belief and strength of previous years and experiences shone through. A hope and purpose for the future opened up with a personal presence so strong I lit up the room wherever I went. It became infectious and other people wanted this 'sparkle' too.

The effect was so profound that I knew so many other people could benefit from it. I now deliver full Colour Analysis and Image Discovery as a key part of my *Unlocking Your Hidden Confidence* programme, so everyone else can discover their own sparkle.

I consider it my mission to help show women how easy it is to stand up and shine with the skills, knowledge and experiences I have learned over the years to ensure you are taken seriously, attract the clients you want whilst feeling and looking confident.

Conducting business virtually has become a necessity and for some the new 'norm'. The first impression is still important online as it is in person. These 7 Top Tips from my programme will ensure you can take immediate action to *Show Up and Shine online.*

1. Consider what your clothes are saying about you? Are they suitable for the meeting and audience? Do they reflect you and your brand?

2. Avoid wearing the colour black. For most people black has the power to drain colour from their face, leaving them looking pale and older than they really are. In the absence of Colour Analysis consider wearing True Primary Red as it is the only colour to have harmony throughout the colour wheel.

3. If you need to be seen as authoritative, wear a jacket. A jacket will bring structure to your shoulder line.

4. Avoid metallics or busy patterns as they can be a distraction.

5. Consider your cleavage – is it showing? Is it appropriate for the meeting?

6. Accessories – Are they adding impact or distracting? Consider the size and scale of jewellery or scarves in proportion to your body size.

7. Wear a lipstick and smile!

Be your best business card, invest in yourself, it's the best investment you will ever make!

Lara Lauder - The Personal Brand Stylist

Lara is an award winning energetic, creative, Personal Brand Stylist who empowers women to reconnect, lead and sparkle with their own unique presence and talents. As an International motivational speaker, she is known for captivating her audiences and speaks regularly on *How to Unlock Your Hidden Confidence.* She is also a professional member of The Professional Speakers' Association.

An entrepreneur from an early age, Lara knows only too well the power of presenting yourself authentically and the value of reputation. Her experience spans two successful franchises, a global network marketing business, as well as a career in teaching. More recently she mentors business owners to success through positive, powerful, personal branding and by utilising their voice and personal presence to ensure positive impact.

She now unites and empowers women from across the world through the *Sparkle & Shine Club* and is Founder of the *Last Step Before Stage Speakers Academy.*

https://www.laralauder.com

https://www.linkedin.com/in/laralauder

https://www.facebook.com/confidencewithcolour

https://www.instagram.com/lara_lauder

How To Design The Real "Super-Brand" ... The Brand That Is You

Pete Cohen - The Inspirator

"A great life doesn't happen by chance. It happens by design and you have the power to change."

I was recently doing some work with a group of people, who are a part of my coaching community. We were talking and one of them said, "every time we want to do something that is about our growth, we don't really want to do it because there's a part of us that just doesn't want to grow". I was quite shocked by what he said because he's a functional medicine doctor. I thought about this for the whole week and then I had an epiphany. He was right. We don't want to grow. We resist change because we are settlers. We are not hunter-gatherers anymore. I don't know if you know any hunter-gatherers, but then again, they don't live in North London or West Sussex! I mean, there are hunter-gatherers in the world, but they are few and far between, because the hunter-gatherers of the past created a world where we could settle. Hunters would not have gone for a leisurely run or to lift some weights at the gym. That would be ridiculous, as they needed to conserve their energy so they were able to run when they had to.

I can now see clearly what I already knew. I remember reading my favourite book "Think and Grow Rich" many years ago and being fascinated by what the author, Napoleon Hill, had said. He spent 25 years interviewing 500 of the most influential people in industry, from Alexander Graham Bell, to Thomas Edison to Henry Ford and many others. Hill came to the conclusion from all of these interviews that only 2% of the population were indeed driven to succeed. These 2% of people were inspired to really build something that was in front of them. They were so excited about what they were going to create, that how they felt had no bearing on what they did. They had a necessity to act.

Most people are living in a world where everything they do is based on how they feel, and if they don't feel like doing something they will stay put and settle. However, even though we settle and it might feel nice, there is a part of us that still wants more. Basically, human beings are made to grow, evolve and hit the targets we set. We are what the Greeks called *teleological* - we need to achieve to be fulfilled.

There was a time when I got into the 'settle' zone. Business was great and I had been the resident life coach on GMTV for eleven years, a National morning TV show in the UK. My girlfriend at the time Hannah, and I were having the time of our lives and thought we had it all. We were living our dream and could do everything we wanted. But then disaster struck and we were forced to rethink, redesign and reboot everything. Hannah had a major seizure and was rushed into hospital. After many tests and procedures she was given just 18 months to live. This changed everything and we went on an epic adventure as I found a treatment in America that saved her life. Hannah has made a full recovery and has been cancer free now for eight years, but this whole experience gave me a completely different take on health and what it takes to not just be well, but to be magnificent. It got me thinking though... *If being magnificent is so easy to do, why is it that so many millions of people find it so difficult?*

The reason we struggle is that we are fighting a battle in ourselves - the battle to achieve, versus the choice to stay where we feel nice and comfortable. As soon as we get comfortable we develop a horrible disease that I call *excusitis*. This is inflammation of the excuse-making gland, when we say things such as *I just don't feel like it* or *I don't feel like it today, I'll do it tomorrow*. And tomorrow comes and guess what, you have an even greater dose of excusitis. The time has come for us to go from being a settler to being a hunter-gather again, regardless of how we feel.

But what has this got to do with you and your brand? Well your brand needs energy, especially if it's going to become a Super Brand. It needs evolving and for you to take you and your business to new heights, there are going to be times when you don't feel like it, or you come across a huge unforeseen adversity like a virus that takes the world down by storm.

All that matters is what you think about YOU and your brand. Personally, I love everything about my brand. *Mi365* stands for everything I represent. The *Mi* is all about everyone's individual life. It stands for doing a 360 in your life and working on developing yourself for 365 days. My vision is to build a global revolution of 10 million people who have gone from a life of chance to an extraordinary life by design. I am my brand and I live and breathe it. I am obsessed with it and everything I do is about building it. At the heart of it is coaching people to be what they can be so they close the gap between who they are being and who they are capable of being with their health and energy, their relationships and their wealth, work and service. All of these need attention and design. But without doubt, health and energy comes first - especially if you want to build something powerful, profitable and magnificent.

At the heart of everything is energy and that's what your brand needs. The fire cannot go out and I want to help and inspire you with this by sharing with you the Magnificent 7 Steps To Health and Wellbeing.

Your brand needs you to:

- Eat right

- Drink right

- Think right

- Move right

- Talk right

- Sleep right

- Poo right

There is no magic bullet to health, energy and wellness, but I promise you that your brand is calling you to have an abundance of energy. It was Abraham Maslow who said, "What man can be, he must be." Your brand must be full of energy if you are going to build it and take it to where it's capable of being. Think about your audience and customers and how you want them to feel about you and your brand. Do you not want them to be energised by you? The only way to have energy is to work on the Magnificent 7. It's an inside job and no one can do it for you, but there is help at hand.

The intention with the Magnificent 7 is to create a system that is resistant to disease, able to self-repair and able to respond with energy to the challenges we face in growing ourselves, and our brand. Taking care of your health is a courageous act. But it can't be an act, it has to be a habit and that's what Aristotle said 2500 years ago. Think about the people you buy into. Why do you do this? Is it something to do with their energy?

It takes courage to commit to building a successful business and so too does living your life on purpose and taking care of the fundamentals. What is your purpose? Is your purpose not to make a difference to other people? It all starts with energy and movement. If you want things to move on every level, then you need to move. In fact, our brains reward us when we move, by secreting the chemicals that make us feel good. If you feel good, you are more likely to act good. If you feel great, then guess what? And what if you feel inspired? You get the picture.

Martin Luther King Jr. once said that the most important question we could ask is *What can we do for others.* I agree to some extent, but I would like to say that even more important is what could we do for ourselves that would give us more energy and greater health, so we can serve others better.

Gandhi had some wisdom around this when he said, "Be the change that you would like to see in the world." What does the person you need to become look like? What part will the The Magnificent 7 play?

Here are the fundamentals of the Magnificent 7 to Super Charge You and Your Brand ...

Eat Right

You need to eat super-clean – and everything you eat 'counts' on this score – with nutrient-dense foods whenever you can. The majority of your diet should be plant-based and at least 50% of this should be green, leafy vegetables if you want to give your energy and creativity a super boost.

Drink Right

The human body is made up of two-thirds water. It is the most fundamental and essential component in our system. It is essential for the effective functioning of just about every part of your body from brain function to detoxification. If you want to thrive rather than just survive, get plenty of pure water into your system.

Think Right

Everything that is showing up in your life comes down to

the choices you make. So, when it comes to health, you need to think healthy. When it comes to success, you need to think success. Our thoughts precede our actions and our actions lead to results. So, if you change your thinking, this will provoke different actions and as a result, will lead you to the results you want to have.

Move Right

Life is motion. If you aren't moving then you are dying. One of the most common causes of death in the Western world is inactivity. The human body is designed to do just one thing – and that's to move!

Talk Right

It is also worth thinking about the way you talk to yourself. The inner self-talk that you have going on in your head can inspire and motivate you, or it can be like a duck, quacking constantly in your head. Talk to yourself as you would talk to your best friend and be kind.

Sleep Right

Current advice is that we should all get eight hours a night – and an alarming number of us don't even manage that. The fact is, if you are not recharging your body every day with at least eight hours of sleep per night, you are running on stress hormones and there is only so long your body can do that before it starts to burn out and turn into disease.

Poo Right

Elimination is a vital process of your body. It's the way it detoxifies and expels waste that your body does not need. If your body is holding onto sh*t you don't need anymore, it's going to compromise every element of your health whilst all the toxins that shouldn't be there start to get into your blood and each of your vital organs. If you want to create the perfect outer environment for your business to flourish, you need to create the perfect inner environment first.

Now you understand the Magnificent 7, what is your next step? First and foremost, spend a few minutes deciding what *good* would look like for each of these seven areas.

Track how well you observe each of the Magnificent 7 (score them on a scale of 1 to 5). Start looking for patterns, both in how one affects the other, (if you sleep right, do you then think right and talk right?) and also how the Magnificent 7 affects other areas of your life.

Use the image to chart your progress.

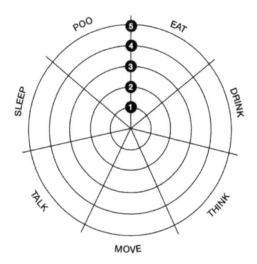

If you want to learn how to be more inspired to take the lead with your health and energy you can download a copy of my book for free, "Inspirators - Leading The Way In Leadership" *https://book.petecohen.com/*

Pete Cohen - The Inspirator

Pete is the international best selling author of 19 books, award winning motivational speaker, coach to the stars and Founder of the Global revolution Mi365, which has been designed to liberate 10 million lives from living life by chance to an extraordinary life by design.

Over the last 30 years, Pete has been the ignition and inspiration behind some of the world's greatest change makers, supporting everyday people through to Olympic Champions and high flying business executives to achieve their greatest human potential. He knows exactly how to motivate people to close the gap between where they are and where they want to be with their health, wealth and happiness and has made it his life's mission to do so.

You will regularly find Pete speaking on the Global stages, presenting on TV and transforming lives through his Podcast - The Inspiration Revolution. If you want to live your life by design rather than chance, Pete is certainly The Inspirator to take you there.

https://book.petecohen.com

Standing Up In Your Own Hallelujah!
... Why YOUR Voice Matters In Your Business

Gayle Edwards - The Personal Brand Disruptor

"Knowing who you are, what you do, how you do it and the impact it has, will create a shift in you, your business and your clients like no other resource, tool or technique can!"

There is something really disarming about not being able to express yourself in an unfamiliar situation with unfamiliar people. As adults we feel fear, anxiety and can be paralysed by the uncertainty of what is going on, when we are not able to articulate what we really want to say. Now imagine that situation as a three-year-old child. That three-year-old was me!

Until that point, I had lived a quiet existence. As an only child, I spent my time at home being looked after by various relatives, as my Mum, a Caribbean Immigrant, was constantly working to establish a lifestyle that would provide me with comfort and opportunity. Relatives, who found it easy to ignore me due to my trouble-free nature. I was comfortable... and quiet until my first day at school.

Suddenly, I was thrust into a strange environment with hordes of people and so many noisy children – all whizzing around me. I was terrified and spent the entire day in tears. Not talking was not due to anything physical. I just had not yet mastered the art of putting sentences together. So instead of being exposed,

I said nothing, aside from the odd yes… no came a lot later in life! Finally, at aged four, the relationship between reading and communication clicked. So much so, I became obsessed with learning new words, their definitions, and different ways of expressing myself.

By the time I was six I was a 'Free Reader', i.e I had gone through all of the guided reading books and was able to pick whichever book I wanted from the shelf. My first taste of empowerment. Story Time became my favourite part of the day. I was able to lose myself in the adventures of The Famous Five and Milly Molly Mandy whilst honing my investigative skills with Emile and The Detectives.

I was experiencing freedom for the first time and loved it!

Though emboldened with my reading choices at school, there were still parts of my life where I couldn't express myself. I had this ever-expanding vocabulary but didn't feel confident to use it to talk about my hopes and dreams or to cultivate a friendship with a best friend! Then there was that question that adults like to ask children… what do you want to be when you grow up? I was always a bit shy to answer because I wanted to be a Traffic Warden. I really liked the idea of giving people tickets. Of course, I had no concept, at the time, of what that ticket actually was. I was totally enamoured with the idea of being the one that gives the ticket. I had no idea how that feeling of wanting to *be the one* was going to inspire my entrepreneurial journey.

I often say to my clients *the clue is in the who.*

- Who are you really?

- Who are you destined to be?

- Who do you need to become in order to create the legacy, business or success that you want?

The Clue Is In The Who!

As I navigated through my life and became more vocal, I realised that whilst I had found my voice, it was very different to the voices of those around me. I knew I wasn't going to follow the traditional route of finding a job and committing to it for the next 30 or 40 years. My intuition was already telling me I didn't need to sell my soul to somebody else in order to be successful. I knew that from the first moment I walked up to that 'Free Readers Shelf' and picked my own book!

What I hadn't yet put together was all the little clues that led me to where I am today. Right now, we are in a world where communication is key. A world that is not that different to when I was that three-year-old girl desperately wanting to make myself heard and understood. This is exactly where so many Entrepreneurs, Business Owners and even Corporate Leaders are today - they are that three-year-old girl. The world is changing, your market, your industry is becoming more and more crowded each day. The *noise* of new technologies and services is getting louder. Disruptors are entering your space and turning tried and tested formats and processes on their heads and creating outstanding results and outcomes in dizzying speeds.

Not knowing how to communicate to make our voice stand out puts us on the back foot. I am eternally grateful to have had an early lesson in the power of voice because that has been the fuel in my Personal Branding and Communications business. When I decided, over 20 years ago, to be an Entrepreneur, I knew I had to be the person that was going to help other people to find not just their voice but also their reason for being.

Metaphorically, I am the one that gives Disruptive Entrepreneurs the ticket to their authentic self and to their freedom of being exactly who they are supposed to be in their business. Their ticket is marked with confidence, clarity and commitment to showing up and serving their audience with authenticity, integrity and passion.

Through my *Standing Up In Your Own Hallelujah* process, they are able to move past the confusion and discover what foundations they are building or have built their business on. As we work through the *Standing Up In Your Own Hallelujah* process we start with Identity – the non-negotiable fundamentals in your business.

Remember the clue is in the who!

Times have changed, and the online world has accelerated the shift into the Human to Human economy. An economy where communication and connection are more important than ever. Integrity and authenticity are not the new words on the business block for nothing! Personal Branding maximises our success in this H2H economy - it amplifies our values, our vision, and our voice – our voice to others but, most importantly our voice to ourselves!

Funny enough, most Entrepreneurs think about their business name, logo, business cards, website... i.e the image but spend virtually no time on the values or identity of both the business and themselves as the business owner! Whilst image is important and is part of the process, we don't tackle it until towards the end of the process! Entrepreneurs who have worked with me usually end up changing something in their existing marketing communications because it no longer reflects their voice and it feels out of alignment.

When you are in a period of reflection, especially if challenges are showing up in your business such as not enough clients, too many low value sales, lack of opportunities and many more, this is the starting point to finding the answers. You don't have to be a scared three-year-old trying to figure it out. You can be the person that commits to showing up in your business. You can commit to *Standing Up In Your Own Hallelujah* by getting fully grounded in your identity, explore the other elements within the process, including impact, get to know your true voice because one of the things I have seen numerous times and know for sure is that when you discover and use your true voice – others listen!

If you're reading this book and thinking you already have an ok business without all this personal branding stuff then great! However, if you want an outstanding business that creates legacy and has a profound impact on the people you serve then keep reading and take action. Disruptive Personal Branding is an inside job. It is not about the pretty pictures or the logo it's not even about the speech. It's all about you and as we go through the process you also learn how to have fun in your business and how to create campaigns and products easily yet distinctively! However, don't let the fun and ease mislead you – we go deep! Becoming an authority in your market will provide you with crystal clear clarity that is so ingrained within you that you become the roots of your own oak tree.

We've all heard the saying, *Out of little acorns grow mighty oaks*. Disruptive Personal Branding is how you start to grow into that mighty oak from your little acorn. Over the past 20 years, every client that has implemented the 4 Pillars of Disruptive Personal Branding (including the secret 5th Pillar) is now *Standing Up In Their Own Hallelujah* and has experienced a shift that has upscaled their business, their profits and, most importantly, amplified their voice and positioned them as a Global Market Leader.

To find out more about Gayle Edwards and her trail blazing *Standing Up In Your Hallelujah* process and the 4 Pillars of Personal Branding, you can download her virtual business card at *bit.ly/BrandYouBiz* which contains access to her website and all social media platforms. Additionally, please feel free to join her complimentary Facebook group, The Disruptor Club by going to *bit.ly/DisruptorClub*.

Gayle Edwards - The Personal Brand Disruptor

Gayle Edwards is an International, award-winning Personal Brand and Positioning Strategist, Author and Speaker who works with Entrepreneurial Disruptors to help them build their identity and authority within their marketplace!

As the CEO of Brand You Consultancy Ltd, Gayle uses her 30 plus years' experience in Marketing, Branding, Communications, Training and Coaching to help Entrepreneurs and Corporate Professionals to boost their identity, create more impact, extend their influence and sharpen up their image.

Gayle is also the creator of the trailblazing *Standing Up In Your Own Hallelujah* Personal Branding process.

Gayle has delivered keynote speeches for organisations as well as national and international conferences.

Gayle interviews Entrepreneurial Disruptors from around the globe as the host of *The Dare To Be Awesome Podcast Show* and co-host of *The Entrepreneurs Sushi Club* podcast. Gayle also founded *Daring Daughters*, a soon to be launched social enterprise focussed on encouraging young women into entrepreneurship.

bit.ly/BrandYouBiz

bit.ly/DisruptorClub

Going Global From My Living Room... Why Success Is All About You

Amanda Frolich - The Funtivity Expert

"Reach for the stars but don't be blinded by the lights."

I had just delivered my best party ever. It wasn't for Brangelina or the Beckhams. Nor was it at The Atlantis on The Palm in Dubai. It was right here in front of my cream leather sofa, between the four walls that make up my living room.

I had Nana dancing in Italy and Uncle Marc dancing in Bangkok. The sheer joy on the faces of the birthday boys was priceless. If you had have told me that I would be able to change lives from my living room thirty years ago when I first started out as a children's sports assistant, I'd never have believed you. In fact, I'd have laughed in your face.

Back then, success was about growth and numbers; getting my name out there and being as 'BIG' as a name as I could possibly be. I've been round the world and back again on a journey that's been as bumpy as it has been long and I can now tell you, with complete certainty, that success is all about YOU. My 'one man band' is where I keep coming back to and it turns out that there really is no place like home.

Trust Your Gut

My *light bulb moment* came back in 1991 whilst shopping in the Wembley Ikea, London. I stood there, playing with the ears, nose and tail of the toy bunny I had in my hand. There, in an instant, Amanda's Action Club was born. Ealing Council, my employer at the time, had just paid for me to do a Movement and Music course. The idea was I'd play some nursery rhymes in the leisure centre and the local pre-schoolers and their parents would dance around. To put this in context, these were the days when pre-school activities consisted of little more than musty church halls and a few boxes of hand me down toys.

Once a week, mums (yes, it was very much about mums then) endured the instant coffee, Rich Tea biscuits (if they were lucky) and long-life milk, whilst the toddlers burned off some energy. Back then, no one was providing a daily schedule of activities for three-year olds. Tell parents then that a plethora of language, art and coding classes were on the way and they'd have thought you utterly insane!

Anyway, back to the bunny. The movement and music course taught me the importance of getting children and their parents active, about shared moments and experiences between parent and child. It was all well and good, but as we all know, the attention span of most pre-schoolers can be compared to that of a gnat! OK maybe that's a little harsh. Between six and ten minutes is around the time you've got to enthral, engage and entertain. Pre-Ikea I'd been playing *Hop Little Bunnies* and we'd all dance around excitedly, but after a few songs, little minds would start to wander and I'd lose control.

I'd been trying to work out how, in my local hometown's run-down community centre with just my stereo and I, how I could captivate my audience for longer. Suddenly, bunny in hand, I had the answer. Props! I was so eager to test out my theory, I bought the lot and the very next day went to my class armed with my bag of bunnies. The children were thrilled, as was I.

I knew, right there and then, that my magic formula of entertainment, education and exercise was a winning one.

From that moment on I trusted my gut. If I felt it was right in the pit of my stomach, then it probably was. This 'feeling' has rarely let me down.

Reach For The Stars

The bunnies soon multiplied and were joined (in the back of my rusty old van) by a multitude of buses, 'steering wheels,' sea creatures, shakers and drums. If there was a prop, there was a story to be told and a window out onto this big wide world to be opened. I loved what I was doing and wanted to share it with as many people as possible, but I knew, that to do that, it had to be perfect.

So I worked and I worked to make it so.

No longer content to play other people's music, I decided to write my own songs to help kids learn the things they needed to know. I invested thousands in these albums. Thousands of pounds I didn't really have. I reached for the stars and I was determined to get there. By now, I was doing classes all over London and one day in Wandsworth, a mum asked if I could possibly do a birthday party? Children then were generally content with a few friends in the garden, some butterfly cakes and candles. They didn't know anything else. Having an entertainer was a big deal and this deal sent me stratospheric.

My first celebrity party was for Brand Beckham. I got a call from Victoria's mum who asked, "What is your fee?". "David and Victoria want you to entertain the kids at their World Cup Party." I didn't name my price. "How could I?", I thought, as this is all for charity. In fact, I pretty much ran the whole event for free. Mark Owen from Take That, followed by Amanda Holden, Peter Jones, Katie Price and even 'Brangelina' came calling by referral – often repeatedly. I did their parties – at my standard rate – and hoped that one of them would give me a mention, but sadly it wasn't to be. Even those who praised me in their weekly newspaper columns failed to name me by name. I didn't let that hold me back though and I was soon at capacity. Working seven days a week, reaching burnout and finally deciding that it needed to be about more than just me.

Franchising Failures

Franchising was not to be. I didn't know it at the time, but I wasn't going to go global. I'd never crack America. I wouldn't even make it in Margate, England. I tried, oh boy, did I try. But I failed. Had I taken the advice of my mentor, Sammy Blindell, back then and trusted my gut, I'd never have set foot down this long and very windy road, but I did and it's shaped me.

First came Fiona, (name changed for obvious reasons) a franchising guru, or so I'd been told. £25,000 later I had a website and 225 pages of franchising documents. Not one of those pages held water.

Next came a total bill of £150,000 for franchise consultancy fees from a company who claimed to be the best in the business. "You can't be Amanda's Action Club" they told me, "you'll never sell a franchise to anyone but an Amanda."

Stupidly, I believed them.

They tried to woo me in Wuhan, China. They wined and dined me. The food on my plate left as bad a taste in my mouth as the deal on the table. Next it was Turkey and then the Philippines and whilst my experience in Asia was beyond incredible, the same can't be said for any of my forays into franchising. Deals abandoned, bank balance in the red and finally, finally, the realisation that I was better off alone.

Coming Full Circle

During the franchising years I didn't stand still. I couldn't afford to. I was top of my game as an entertainer and determination ran through my veins. "They need you in Dubai," a client insisted, "their parties are out of this world, but they've got no soul." So off I went.

While my husband sunned himself at The Hilton, I ran around, suited and booted, knocking on doors. Straight to the top I went of Time Out Dubai (for publicity), Jumeirah Beach Hotel and Atlantis on The Palm. I got column inches, the gigs I craved and the chance to entertain at one of the Middle East's most prestigious venues. Landing in Heathrow I was elated. Six days before I was due to fly back out to host the event of my career, I found myself in a mangled heap, in the middle of Chiswick High Road. A car had run me down after one of my classes. Both of my legs were as shattered as my dreams. I picked myself up (as I always do), went back to Dubai, and achieved what I set out to. Nothing would stop me. But there, on The Palm, came the realisation, finally, that global domination was not for me.

Skip forward five years and another light bulb moment...

This time, it was the one hanging from my living room ceiling. It just smacked me in the head in the middle of one of my daily Zoom classes. Embarrassing yes, painful, yes, but I couldn't care less. I'm the happiest I've ever been and I feel the most successful I've ever been too.

Back at Ground Zero is where I belong. I'm doing what I do best – being me. Getting kids and their parents active from my living room to theirs. Giving them music, movement and memories. Without trying to I've got a global audience - thousands joining in with Action Amanda at Home.

If the 2020s taught me one thing, it's to be true to yourself, respect your roots and success will follow. I'm home and this is where I'll stay today, tomorrow and beyond!

Amanda Frolich - The Funtivity Expert

Amanda Frolich is an award winning celebrity children's entertainer and CEO of Amanda's Action Club, the world's most fun, physical development concept teaching preschool children how to be healthy and active from an early age.

Having spent 28 years working within the early years sector she was invited by the Children's Activity Association to become the Children's First Champion in Parliament, encouraging policy-makers to put children first at the heart of all decision-making.

Her global animation TV series featuring Action Amanda on different missions to create a world of endless possibilities and adventure, is well on its way to achieving Amanda's life-long impact vision and this Wonder Woman is certainly one for you to watch!

https://www.amandasactionclub.co.uk

https://www.facebook.com/amandasactionclub

instagram.com/actionamanda

Speak Your Story, Speak Your Truth... How To Authentically Speak Up, Show Up, And Blow Up Your Brand

Anne Hayes - The Empowerment Queen

"Love and Community provide the channel for our deepest pain to be released, so that our authentic expression can be unleashed."

I stood there, my body quivering from head to toe. My wrist was actually flip flopping from side to side, and I almost dropped the mic I was holding in my hand. *Am I really doing this? Am I crazy to think that me, a middle-aged white female, is going to attempt to freestyle in public, for the first time in her life?*

Heck, I had just started writing rhymes again just about a year ago, after years of shelving what I loved to do as a kid. I must be out of my mind! My breathing started to quicken, and my chest began to tighten just a little bit as I listened to what seemed like the deafening din of local, well-respected emcees chatting it up in the crowd. It didn't help that I was standing under what appeared to be a supernova in the making; lights so bright that I thought maybe a pair of sunglasses on this cold, dreary evening might have helped. I stood there, visible and vulnerable like a naked fish on the end of a big fat hook.

I wavered between utter terror and exhilarating excitement as the DJ asked me for "my beat". "Oh, yeah, right," I answered. "I was planning to do a freestyle. Do you happen to have something you can pull up for me?" *REAAALLLY???* I screamed inside. You show up, and you have the nerve to ask the DJ to dig up some random beat???!!!! The DJ gave me a subtle shrug and flashed a look of stunned amazement.

"Ok, Mama G, that's what you call yourself, right? I think I have something for you."

The crowd was actually a small gathering that evening, thank goodness! As the music began, I watched my sister and my brother-in-law look at me in supportive anticipation. "Do it. Do it! You got this!" Well, the heavens must have opened up, angels must have landed, and someone else may have even taken over my body, I kid you not! It was like Anne Hayes left the house and Mama G showed up to kick some "lyrical with the spiritual" a$$! I crushed it! I was honestly so amazed at myself! For someone who had faced death hundreds of times, if I were to have made even a peep, it was a huge victory. It would be a bit of a journey, however, before I realized just how I believed I was meant to use this gift.

Fortunately, this unfolded with ease and a little bit of patience as I continued to heal from years of sexual abuse as a child. As in most cases of child abuse, I felt disempowered. I was sworn to secrecy by my abuser who alluded to my subsequent death if I were to ever share what was going on. Hence, I lost my voice. I also began the practice of locking down my pain deep inside while I screamed for help and attention in other ways. I exhibited all the tell-tale signs of trauma. I had temper tantrums quite often, even as a teenager. I was negative, I had tremendous rage, debilitating OCD, extreme anxiety, and often pinched, scratched, punched and bit myself. To make matters worse, I experienced night terrors and rarely slept. I wet the bed until I was nine and felt the shame of this.

Needless to say, my confidence was shaken, I suffered from low self-esteem, and over time, became deeply depressed and suicidal.

Looking back, I realized that what ultimately kept me alive was my family. As intolerable as I believe I was, I always knew that I had a home. Along with this safety net, I also found many creative ways to express myself. I drew, sketched, made up dances and skits, wrote stories, poetry and songs. I was a very imaginative child, and I believe this helped to save me, as it allowed me to create my own World. This early creativity would eventually weave its way back into my branding as the core of my business, with almost instantaneous results.

Before then, I thought I was meant to travel the world as a renowned rapper. Nope, I soon realized that dream was a bit too steeped in my need to validate my worth from the attention of others. I did NOT want to fall into that trap! I then thought it was to perhaps teach Hip Hop Yoga to inner-city teens. That was fun, allowed me to craft some fun Hip Hop playlists, but that didn't seem to go anywhere either. And so I kept pursuing the "dream", so to speak, with the promise of abundant wealth.

I began to participate in masterminds and to hire high level speaking and business coaches. With each experience, my creative side and my love for rapping seemed to be "pushed to the back", like who was I to think I could make money with that. As if that wasn't enough, I was told again and again that I would not be able to make any money with teens as my identified demographic. Back to adults and a too general branding that claimed that I was going to, like thousands of others, *provide transformational programs for the individual to achieve breakthrough results in both life and business.* Big, FAT YAWN. Of course, I went with it, since that was what the *branding expert* back then told me.

Finally, as I mentioned previously, my core genius showed itself. My unique purpose unfolded in amazing clarity when I had the courage to show up completely and unabashedly as ME; me with a passion for music beautifully synthesized with a passion to empower and inspire those teens that were once me!

And so how does one go about speaking out and speaking one's truth as a way to heal and to help heal others?

First of all, to reiterate, it involves much more than someone saying, *just be positive* or *change your attitude, and you'll feel better.* Trust me, I knew I was negative when I was negative, and I didn't want to be! It only shamed me and further nibbled away at what little self-esteem I had left at the time! I needed to address the root cause and to release that root cause, like pulling up the most stubborn weeds that had overrun my most amazing garden of life! That's the foundation! From there, there are three basic principles I have come up with that will ensure ongoing healing and transformation.

Simply put, they are:

1. Find a Community

2. Show up, and

3. Start sharing

Why FIND A COMMUNITY?

Because a community offers a sense of belonging. It reminds us that we are not alone. It provides us with support, encouragement, feedback, and an opportunity for growth in a safe environment. That's why I love the Brand Builders Club, as I have finally found a tribe that packs my parachute in the way I need it most. I love that even the Founder of it, Sammy Blindell, is so involved. She fully encouraged me to brand myself the way I've known that I needed to brand myself all along and since I stepped into that brand, my business has flourished. When you have faith in what you are doing and you surround yourself with others who are going in the same direction, you cannot fail. There is a reason that many animals of prey travel in packs and herds. The idea of a lone wolf is a sad one, indeed, and not the existence I believe anyone wants to have. I think we'd all prefer what has been termed, *Herd Immunity*... together, we are stronger and can fight off any disease of the mind or the spirit!

Next, SHOW UP!

Yes, once you have taken the first step, take the next step, and keep going! You have found that community, and now, all you have to do is show up! Showing up means you are choosing to embrace life, to go on living. It means you are willing to create the next greatest version of yourself every time! Furthermore, when you show up, you provide opportunities for yourself to become more deeply integrated into the community of which you have chosen to be a part. You connect, and you create bonds that uplift you!

Finally, START SHARING!

Share your story; tell others who you are, what you believe in and what you don't believe in! Know that you will inspire many! Know that some may not agree with how you show up based on their own belief systems and their own experiences. No worries. Keep sharing, because you will continue to inspire most, and you will grow and expand from the rest! Furthermore, the more you share, the more you will build your confidence to share your authentic truth in your own unique way. Most importantly, you will begin to realize, bit by bit, that you are in fact, completely safe in doing so! This is when it really gets fun! Your inspiration will flow with greater ease, more amazing opportunities will show up (as you show up!), and you will have so much fun doing it all! Your dreams will seemingly blow up overnight, and you will begin to truly FEEL what it is to experience "KICKA$$ HAPPYNESS"!

How do I know this works? Just ask those young, talented artists who have done just that and who now lead and inspire others.

Anne Hayes - The Empowerment Queen

Anne (aka Mama G) is a speaker, author, poet, inspirational rapper and the CVO of Kicka$$ Happyness. Having spent eight years as a new entrepreneur with a desire to share unique strategies and tools to heal and transform others, it wasn't until she began sharing her own personal story in the form of rap that the magic began to appear. This passionate form of expression empowered her to create a unique set of programs that provide a sense of community for teens to overcome negative challenges and influences through the creative arts, so they live more positive, fulfilling lives.

With decades of experience working with teens in a variety of settings, Anne is unofficially credited with saving many lives, including that of her own teenage daughter.

As a powerful liaison between parents, community leaders, and teens, she intends on saving a lot more lives with her natural, passion-driven, non-conventional approach.

https://annehayes360.com

anne@kickasshappyness.com

Conscious and Persistent Courage... How To Create A Sparkling Presence On The Stage of Your Life And Business

Wilma van Dartel - The Conscious Courage Leader

"Bring your Conscious Courage to the world and together we can inspire others around the world to do the same. Imagine that!"

Nowadays business is being done a different way. Business owners are having to be more visible than ever before to capture the attention of new clients, finding new and inventive ways to get in front of them. People are still only spending money with people they know, like and trust. But with so much distraction online now, we are having to be more courageous in the way we show up for them to find us.

People are now doing business with strangers all over the world that they have never met before, but still one thing remains... They want to get to know the person behind the brand before they consider spending money with them. But how do you do that if you no longer live on the doorstep of your ideal clients?

So many entrepreneurs plunge into all kinds of training to develop their skills, such as how to get good at marketing online, how to blog, how to vlog and how to present themselves on their social media profiles. They make excellent plans around how to execute it all so they can make the big impact they dream of making with their superpower. But then… nothing happens. Not a single blog or vlog gets published, or it lacks the heartbeat it needs to gain traction. In my experience, this is because they forgot one very important detail in their grand plan … to work on their personal barriers.

You can easily get ahead of your competitors if you are willing and ready to look at your personal obstacles. In fact, the most courageous thing you can do is take on the very things that withhold you from being the solution provider that your dream prospects and clients are really looking for. If you don't do something about the fears that are holding you back from being seen and if the real YOU doesn't show up to the conversation, then it's highly likely that they are going to turn to those of your competitors who do. You have an obligation to work on yourself as much as you are expecting others to work with you and the time to do that is now. Not only for yourself, but to create the impact on all the lives you want to touch as well.

The worlds needs you and it needs you now!

The fear of being seen is a fear that I used to know only too well. All throughout my childhood I was bullied and excluded because of the port wine stain on my face. I was a pretty happy teenager however, and although I was never the most popular girl in the class, I did pretty well and had lots of friends.

Nevertheless I was insecure about myself, which in itself isn't that weird as many teenagers tend to be insecure. But when I was in my final year of high school, I applied for a corporate secretary education to get a job that was guaranteed when I graduated. I had an intake meeting with a very stout woman; typically dressed in a pink twinset, pearl necklace and her hair in a Grace Kelly roll. I remember thinking how pretty she was. We had a good conversation until, out of the blue, she asked me why I thought I could become a secretary *you know, with your face!* I was just 16, and that comment hit me hard! I just wanted the earth underneath me to open itself up and swallow me.

From that moment on I made an unconscious decision that no one would ever condemn me on the results of my work or my personal presentation again based on my face. I never applied for a job face to face anywhere again and focused instead on getting jobs through employment agencies based on my skills. I always did a great job, so employers quickly asked me to join them in permanent employment. But I didn't realise then what I know now... I was always focusing so much on doing things perfectly to make up for my appearance that I never thought my work was good enough. This made me procrastinate and I adopted a fear of failure and being judged, that unconsciously forced me to spend way more time on things than I needed to so they would be perfect.

Unsurprisingly this totally exhausted me.

It was my way of living back then and I created a good, happy and successful life with all the normal ups-and-downs that everyone experiences from time to time. I was married for a long time and gave birth to three beautiful daughters. I even got on stage to sing and entertain people to push myself out of my comfort zone! All of this until my last job.

After yet another reorganisation in the company my last Manager had no interest in what I was good at and tried to change me into something I'm definitely not. So I worked harder and harder, but whatever I did it was never good enough. Even the things I am an expert in were no longer good enough and after a short period of time I was on the brink of a burn-out. Another reorganisation was coming and bam... I was made redundant and lost my job.

Looking back on that time, it was the best thing that could happen to me! It didn't feel like it at the time though as it never does, but after looking back at my life from a birds eye view I realised that all of the perfectionism and procrastination walls I had built were as an antidote to that dreadful experience at the corporate secretary education intake meeting. That appalling experience had destroyed me mentally and emotionally.

I was hiding behind a perfectly self-built wall AND... nevertheless I was still performing, singing and entertaining on stage to the pleasure of both the audience and myself. 'How interesting' I thought!

I realised I could support others to break through their own barriers, because we all have our own obstacles, each in our own way, which withhold us to manifest who we really are. I became aware that in order to reinforce others, I had to work on myself first because I'm the only one who can do that. No one can do that for me. So, I did and finally I took my future into my own hands by starting my own business. Knowing what I know now, I worked the other way around...

I worked on my personal blocks first and then I honed the skills and techniques I needed to show up and shine on the stage of my business. Make no mistake, the other way around doesn't make it easier! It's really a combination of learning skills and techniques AND working on yourself. Only then can you make the impact you want to make and only then you can make a difference to the world with your solution!

So after many decades I realised that a lack of self worth and perfectionism had almost taken me down. My excuse is that I didn't know. I didn't know that I had fled from one disaster of not being worthy into another... perfectionism. Although I had managed to lead my life with it for decades by hiding my inner self, in the end it haunted me. I understand that you are probably unconscious of things that withhold you to shine on the stage of your own life too and this will be affecting your business in a negative way. Most people, like I was, are unconscious of this. But after reading this, your excuses no longer apply! Therefore I'm going to share with you how you can do it in a better way than I did.

First of all, don't be afraid of fear. Fear protects you from danger. It can make you run, stop, think, feel, listen, hide and take measures. This is essential to avoid or escape dangerous and even life-threatening situations. But when fear controls your life in everything you do and withholds you from trying to explore new things, then, sooner or later, you have to recognize and face your fears. There's no other option, because at some point in your life you will hit that wall as I did. Facing your fears consciously is the only way to grow, become self-confident, happier and have more success in both your life and your business. So regularly take time for yourself and become aware of what you actually think, feel and do. Look at yourself from a distance. Yes that's necessary, just like breathing, eating and sleeping is. Only when you are conscious of how things are can you make a choice:

1. You are totally satisfied with the way your situation is and you want to keep it that way. So you keep doing what you always did and therefore keep getting the results you always got. That's fine! My advice for you is to investigate if and where there is any room for improvement?

2. Somehow you knew it deep down already... you want things to be different! In that case you have to do things differently in order to get the different results you want. So, make an inventory of what you want to change and maybe add something new. Create a priority list out of that. Then list what you practically need to reach those changes.

And then comes the most important thing, for which I offer you my formula of:

Conscious Wanting = T + F > C and D...

Conscious Wanting = conscious *Thinking* (T) + conscious *Feeling* (F) leading to conscious *Choices* (C) and conscious *Doing* (D).

I use this formula in mentoring sessions with my clients. It helps you to rethink, re-evaluate and stay on your path of change.

It supports you to create a bigger impact, become happier and more successful both in your life and your business. But mind you, whatever you choose, 1 or 2, or something in between, everything is okay because you made a conscious choice and that takes courage! Courage to face your fears and break through them.

Plans with the highest success rates consist of conscious goals that are matched with conscious beliefs, conscious values and conscious identity. The longer you wait to work on what might hold you back personally, the longer it will take for you to shine on the stage of your services and products...

Believe me, you working on yourself will make all the difference!

Working with perfectionists like you became my mission in 2018 when I joined the Brand Builders Club. I experienced myself that you can achieve so much more than what you imagined is impossible when you are consciously courageous about the goals you want to achieve and then surround yourself with others who believe in you to achieve it. I stepped fully into my own skin and became the confident, conscious and courageous woman you see before you now.

When I'm on stage, I bring my whole self to the show and show who I am from inside out. I bring my vulnerability to the stage, along with my happy and joking self that my perfectionism used to squash within me. I rediscovered the adventure of my life and I want that for you too! What I know for sure is this... while your barriers may be different to mine, you, like everyone, deserve to have your own stage in life and in business. So my wish for you is to transform your imperfections into your power and purpose, so that you create a sparkling presence on your own stage.

Bring your Conscious Courage to the world and together we can inspire others around the world to do the same.

Imagine that!

Wilma van Dartel - The Conscious Courage Leader

Wilma van Dartel is an International Speaker, Emcee, Author, Singer, Entertainer and Founder of the Conscious Courage Community.

She knows all about conscious courage, having been born with a port wine stain on her face. She grew up with the paralysing fears of rejection and failure that lead her to building a wall of perfectionism. This started as a young girl when she was rejected for her looks, destroying her emotionally and mentally, forcing her to hide behind a perfectly self-built wall for many decades until she found the conscious courage to step up, show up and stand out.

As the Conscious Courage Leader she now works with perfectionists to show them how to transform their imperfections into power and purpose, so they can create a sparkling presence on the stage of their lives and businesses. Now it's her mission to build a global community for over one million perfectionists who all practice courage with consciousness, so that their impact is greater on all the lives they want to touch.

www.wilmavandartel.nl (in Dutch at the moment)

https://www.facebook.com/groups/ ConsciousCourageCommunity

https://www.linkedin.com/in/wilmavandartel

The Power Of Your Story...
Be Vulnerable And Create Connection

Ruth Driscoll - The Life Liberator

'To Unlock Customer Connection, Your Story is the Key.'

Remember your favourite childhood stories. When you recall them does it conjure up the excitement and pleasure you felt at that time? A good story doesn't simply stay in your mind. It nestles in your heart. But story isn't just for childhood. Story is one of the most useful business tools that you can encounter and offers you an incredible way of communicating with your customers. And here's why.

Story touches your emotions. It pulls you in. You have to stay around to know what happens. A well-told story can make you laugh or it can break your heart. It makes you think or wonder. It can teach you things and fill you with awe. It simplifies and makes sense of complexities. It paints pictures in your mind. When you hear a good story, you often want to share it. You want others to experience the same feeling. When we share, we connect. When you connect with someone through story, they relax and listen.

Our brains easily dismiss logic. Why? Simply because that's not how we operate. Logic is not your friend. Data can, and often will, be challenged. *Lies, damned lies and statistics*, is a phrase popularised by Mark Twain. Story, however, isn't so easy to dismiss. Whether we recognize it or not, we are driven by what we feel. It is in our emotional brains that feelings of trust, loyalty and hope are activated.

That is where unconscious transformational decisions are made.

We are born with our brains hard-wired for story-telling. By the time you were three years old, you had mastered the most powerful tool that mankind has for creating change.

You already understood the principles of story-telling.

So whether you think you can or think you can't, story-telling is an innate skill that you must tap into. In business today it is the best way to create connection with a potential client and nurture a relationship with a customer. Create pictures rather than cold hard facts. You get one chance to grab the attention of that prospective new client. Are you using the most powerful tool you have at your disposal to do that?

Are you using your story?

Little did I know how important story would be in my business. I am The Life Liberator. My mission is supporting those in manipulative, abusive, controlling relationships into empowerment and freedom. To set the context around my story, let me first ask you an important question.

Do you enjoy giving gifts? Of course you do. You are thoughtful about choosing something that you know will please the recipient. It generates a fuzzy, feel-good warmth, watching the joy on their face as they unwrap their gift.

When you enter a romantic relationship, it's rather like you are giving your new partner a gift. Imagine it as a box that you hold in your hand. Into that box you put all the things that are the essence of you. Your love. Your kindness and support. Your sense of fun and joy. Your sexiness, oh-la-la! Your generosity. Your hopes, dreams and plans for the future. Perhaps most of all, your vulnerability.

You offer that gift trusting it will be valued and treasured. As any gift should be.

Here is my story...

I entered a relationship with a man who turned out to be manipulative, abusive and controlling. Slowly he crushed that gift right before my eyes and tossed it aside as something worthless and contemptible. The gift box lay flattened and there was little left of the precious things I put inside.

That is how it feels to be involved with such a partner.

Yet, while I am living with this abusive man, I'm also Headteacher of a challenging inner-city primary school, culturally diverse, situated on an estate where there are gangs with guns and knives; where illegal dog fights take place; a place where poverty haunts people's lives. A scary place to bring up a family. This is a needy, demanding community and to lead it successfully, I draw automatically on qualities of resilience, courage and calm assertiveness. Yet at home I have become someone I don't recognize.

Until that one fateful day when I tell him he has to leave.

"You want me to leave this house!! I'll make sure this house is a wreck by the time I leave! I'll ruin your reputation. I'll make sure you lose your job! Your ugly witch-face will be on every paper in the land!" Words spat at me on foaming beds of spittle.

But the next day he left.

And the story took a new direction.

Recovery from an abusive relationship takes time. My health and my emotional well-being were shattered along with my self-esteem. With sadness, I resigned from my position as Headteacher. Once I had recovered sufficiently, I considered what I should do next. My mentors said, "You should use your experience. All that you went through."

Excuse me! "No way! I'm not using that! I don't want to go back there. I'm ashamed that it happened to me!"

Have you ever been in a situation where it feels like you're being dragged kicking and screaming to do the thing that turns out to be the best thing you ever did? After vehement protest with Sammy Blindell at The Brand Builders Club and lengthy procrastination, The Life Liberator was born. Yes, my advisers were right all the time! I finally realised that my personal and professional experiences meant I was perfectly placed to help others to handle the bullying relationships in their lives.

The power behind my business is my story. I do the thing I never expected I would do. I share my vulnerability and expose my emotional scars. Maybe you are part of my audience, or maybe you're not. Either way, now you know my story, do you feel that you now connect with me at a deeper level? For my audience, hearing my story unlocks the door for them to speak freely about their own situation. Often it will be one about which they have kept silent, possibly for many years. Like me, they felt ashamed. Vulnerability through story is the strongest pillar of my brand in creating connection.

So what is the power of your S.T.O.R.Y?

S - STICKABILITY

Most people forget facts and figures. But everyone remembers a story that resonates with them. Through your story, you linger in your customers' minds. They remember you because they know you. They 'get' you. Guess what! That means you stand out way above your competitors.

T - TRUST

We display vulnerability with those we trust. Usually we are only vulnerable in front of our friends and loved ones. Be open and courageous enough to be vulnerable in front of your potential clients. They will find it so much easier to connect with you. In fact connection is now natural and seamless. The most authentic way to achieve that is through your story.

O - OPTIONS

Do you know who you want to work with? Even more importantly do you know who you don't want to work with? Your story pre-qualifies potential clients. The principles and the integrity of your brand resonate naturally with those who are your ideal client. Those who don't will disqualify themselves without you wasting valuable time finding that out for yourself.

R - REASONS

Your story defines who you are and what you and your brand are all about.

Through your story you display the principles that matter to you and your business. This is so much more powerful than a spreadsheet of facts and figures. You demonstrate those principles in action. Story releases your customer from PowerPointPurgatory. There is a world of difference between telling someone you have integrity and showing them. Your story allows your audience to make up their own minds. Consequently the connection with you runs deeper. Your brand makes sense to a customer who shares your values and is aligned with your story.

Y - YOU

Those who disrespect their customer with false stories don't stay in business very long. The power of story works when you are genuine, authentic and vulnerable. Your brand values are underpinned by the story that shows your customer why you have created this business and why your principles matter to you. Even more powerful is when your customers go out and tell stories about you.

Your story removes barriers. Every story is an opportunity to connect. It's like inviting others into your home. The story creates a whole new context around this relationship. Your customer is now like a guest that you treat with respect and openness. There is nothing to hide. Your customer feels safe and appreciated which means you now enjoy a conversation. They feel emotionally connected. Communication takes place at a more profound level.

That kind of connection creates customer loyalty. And that is what ensures your business thrives.

Ruth Driscoll - The Life Liberator

Ruth Driscoll is an award-winning International public speaker, International best-selling Author, TEDx speaker, powerful trainer, mentor and coach.

Her experiences provide a unique perspective on how to effectively handle manipulative, abusive and controlling people wherever they appear in your life. The damaging influence of those 'difficult' people becomes a thing of the past. As The Life Liberator, she leads those living with manipulative, abusive, controlling relationships at work or at home into empowerment and freedom.

Ruth's past as a Headteacher of a challenging inner-city London primary school before the bullying of an abusive partner caused a complete change to her circumstances. Ruth says, "Those who endure abuse and control at home and/ or at work often feel ashamed and stay silent. By telling my story, it opens the door for others to talk about their own experiences. This is an important starting place to release from that toxic influence."

www.thelifeliberator.org

ruth@thelifeliberator.org

Facebook: Ruth Driscoll - The Life Liberator

LinkedIn: Ruth Driscoll

Twitter: @ruthmdriscoll

Instagram: The_Life_Liberator

Look To The Top of The Mountain And Keep Climbing... Your Challenges Will Be Your Driver

Caroline Purvey - The Feel It To Heal it Specialist

*"Challenges are the drivers that test survivors
to step up not give up."*

"What on earth is going on here?" he said. "Clear these coffee cups, get some air freshener and get these ashtrays out of here. Look at all the boxes lying around. You need to have a real sort out here. Tell your friends to visit you at home when you have time on your hands, not when you are working in your business. Stop playing at it. If you are going into business then be professional about it. Get this place looking like a shop and not a social club." Phew that put me in my place – My dad gave it to me with both barrels that day and that was nearly 38 years ago! It cut to the core. He was right. When he left I cried, not just because my dad rarely ranted and raised his voice like that, but because he was right.

I was a 28-year-old, newly married - for the second time, mum of three. I had always been entrepreneurial. I loved business. The very shop I had bought my own wedding outfit from not a few months before was on the market and for some crazy reason I wanted to take it on. I decided it was time to leave the work I had been doing as a Double-Glazing sales rep anyway. I was the first woman in a man's world with that one, but despite the odds I made my mark. It was however time for change. I went for it and there I was... a retailer!

Having invested a lot of money taking over an existing business, I excitedly dived into the boxes and boxes of stock that came with the sale. The smile soon left my face. I realised half of it would never sell for the price I paid for it, let alone with the mark up! In a flash I realised that I had been naïve. If I was honest it was blind faith and a massive lack of research or planning that left me asking "What have I got myself into?" With the blasting from dad too I really questioned how little I had thought the whole thing through.

I felt in that moment like I was standing at the bottom of an extremely high mountain. If I was going to make a success of what I had invested in and reach the top, there was going to be one hell of a climb ahead. The obstacles seemed to come fast and furious. I had two choices that day – step up or give up. I chose to step up. I brought professionals in to value the stock and fight my claim. The company was called 'Brides and Babies' and I realised that I needed to specialise – make a choice Brides or Babies? Brides won. Be professional. After ten years in retailing I learned many lessons whilst climbing that mountain. The important thing is I have never forgotten them.

All the challenges of my past ventures have been mountains to climb, but I look back and really they have all been practice runs. A chance to deal with challenges that may have seemed insurmountable at the time yet served to be the foundation for something much bigger. In 2011, I took on my biggest mountain yet and after nine years it has at times felt like I have been on a mission to conquer Everest! This business came about from a chance sharing in a yoga class. Before I knew it I had followed my gut to South Africa with ninety-nine people from around the world, learning a practice that to most seemed crazy. However, it was a natural body release to let go of tension and before leaving the course (careful what you wish for too) I vowed to return to the UK and 'make it happen' here.

Always having been a team player I was excited to be part of something global. I returned home with such enthusiasm for the benefits that self-releasing had on a physical, mental and emotional level. I set up TRE UK® (Total Release Experience®) and at the same time I opened my Yoga Centre, which gave me the perfect space to add this extra string to my bow. Never was I one for putting all my eggs in one basket. This was the perfect complement as it fitted with my mission that whoever entered the centre would always leave feeling better than when they arrived. I started to work with clients who knew and trusted me enough to find out more. I was excited, enthusiastic, passionate and compassionate about the sharing and caring with my work. I had a global vision for the future of where I saw it all going. Unexpectedly it was not too long before I started to meet my first challenge:

Challenge No 1

People: Which Side Of The Fence Are They?

In business you will meet two types of people... those who are with you supporting your dream – family, friends, business associates or clients – and those who are not... family, friends, business associates or clients. I soon realised my first big challenge was that the team I wanted to join had a different agenda.

Wow, my curiosity was seen as a threat and there I was on my own again. My enthusiasm was dampened, like a bucket of water on my fire.

I could have wallowed, for my self-esteem felt rather shattered. There I was again – faced with that same choice, step up or give up! I stepped up of course.

Over the years there have been many people on my mountain climb. They have, in different ways, put blockades along my path. But you know I thank them all, for they tested my grit and made me focus on what I totally believed in. This gave me the strength to sidestep them, to stand up to them and keep driving forward.

Take your strength from the good guys around you; the ones that share those words of encouragement or gratitude - especially from clients for how you have helped them on their journey. They are going to give you the fuel to keep climbing. I sometimes have a rare day of self-doubt, but when I read an email from someone saying thank you for changing their life in a way they never thought possible, I smile and say to myself, "Yes - that is why I do what do".

Challenge No 2
You Can't Do It All...

I have learned through trial and error that if your business is going to grow you need to work with others. It became evident that without the right tools in the box, for every step up the mountain there would be 10 back. Yes, it is scary choosing the right people that you can trust, confide and invest in. I have my son Daniel to thank for pushing me out of that mindset. Daniel joined me on my mission and took over tasks he said I should not be doing. He introduced me to Sammy Blindell at The Brand Builders Club. Wow then the challenges started to become different ones.

I was challenged to trust others and learn new ways of doing things. I had to learn how to manage and grow in a way I never would have thought possible, changing my mindset along the way. Sammy and the talented entrepreneurial, positive mindset of the members within her Brand Builders Club didn't just have me walking up the mountain, they had me running up it! The investments in technology, skills and systems have been challenging for sure, but good ones. What we are creating now is because of the tools we have been encouraged to use – which are doing the job of five employees for a fraction of the cost.

If you had told me two years ago that my course could be taught online I would have laughed, in fact to be honest I did! Our course is now online and people the world over can learn they too can 'feel it to heal it'. That global vision is fast becoming a reality. Do your homework invest wisely and invest in the best. Don't try and do it all on your own.

Challenge No 3
Keep It Simple Stupid!

This challenge has been the biggest. Sharing something that to be honest has proven to be more powerful than medicine is baffling. It is all about a muscle in the body you see – the psoas. Yet putting what we teach into words that the Doctors, Psychologists, military, services, inmates and teenagers can understand without compromising our credibility and authenticity has been a challenge like no other.

I like to keep things simple. Trying to wrap something in jargon, science or baffle brains is not always the answer. We convey our message with three simple words – Diamonds, Buckets, and Roller Coasters! When a Doctor says, 'I love your language, it is so easy to share and yet makes so much sense.' You know you have cracked it.

For the first time in eight years the top of that mountain has been my focus and dare I say it, I am starting to see the clouds above. Having overcome my biggest challenges (and there will be more for sure), those challenges have been my biggest drivers. They may well be yours too. Every challenge you have ever had in life, like me, will have prepared you and put you on the path you are now on. Before you go too far up that mountain, be sure that the climb is the very reason you get out of bed every day. With no passion you will have no drive. Your passion is what will be the bulldozer you need drive you through those challenges as you follow your path. Keep climbing and I'll see you at the Top!

Caroline Purvey – The Feel It To Heal it Specialist

Caroline Purvey is an award-winning, bestselling author, International speaker, CEO of TRE UK® and founder of the 'Feel It to Heal It' process.

Caroline is a specialist in her unique programme the Total Release Experience®, which she evolved to release symptoms of stress and trauma where traditional methods have failed. Lives are quite simply transformed through the process and it comes highly recommended by professionals including Doctors, Psychotherapists and Therapists.

Caroline's programme has now been adopted by the Jewish Community, Fire and Rescue Service, the Police Force and the Prison Service, taking this powerful programme to the heart of organisations, families, key workers and every-day people all over the world.

The only Accredited Course of its kind with the FHT, it is delivered through the power of workshops, online courses and intensive 1-2-1 courses.

After an expedition to Malawi in 2018, Caroline took her ripple further afield, by training 19 adults to teach the Total Release Experience® to treat their community. To date over 3,500 challenged children in Africa have been supported to heal their trauma and build their resilience, so they can go on to lead happy healthy lives.

https://treuk.com

caroline@treuk.com

https://www.facebook.com/treuk

Instagram: treuk

If You Don't Like Your Business - Change It! ... The Yawn Factor

Kerry Bartley - The Employment Escape Artist

"No matter what the situation, you have the power to ensure that your safety net, doesn't become your hangman's noose."

Brrrrrrr! The alarm clock is frantically ringing at its usual high intensity, yet I am the complete opposite – low energy. I can scarcely get myself out of bed and, to be honest, I just cannot face another day of monotony. Another long, low paid day at the office filled with thankless task after thankless task. Being at someone else's beck and call. Sitting at my desk long after everyone else, aside from Mickey (the office mouse!) has gone home. My goodness, when, is this actually going to end? At forty I am a long way off retirement so that's not an option yet, but what is the alternative now?

Every single day the routine continues ... resentfully topping up my travel card, cramming myself into what feels like a sardine can, but is actually the London Underground just to arrive at exactly the same spot! As I look at the imposing office building, I can already feel my blood draining, my already low-energy falling even further, leaving no space at all for any oxygen to reach my lungs and give me some much-needed breath. My head hurts – it's going to be one of those days! But one thing I know for sure, is that this living hell has been going on for far too long. I've been playing it safe and now I'm ready to make a change ... regardless.

Looking back, I now realise fear had been holding me. It was fear that kept me safe, but it was also making me fade away, smaller and smaller to a shadow of my former self. I needed to take action but didn't know where to start.

The day it finally happened, I was ready, I had no idea it was going to be that day because it was just like any other mundane day. It's 8pm, as usual, I am sitting alone in the empty office catching up on work whilst Mickey scrambles around. Yet the empty chairs are now telling me a different story. They are telling me that whilst their usual occupants are out living their lives my chair will never be empty because I give everything I have to the mundane!

BAM! Just like that, I realised I was in MY CHAIR! My thoughts swirled like a herd of wildebeest threatening to crush me in their stampede. It was time, I had to get out whilst there was still some hope of a better life. The stampede quickened... stay and be crushed or jump and be free?

That very second, the decision was made, I jumped. Cleared my desk and my locker and never went back. Tomorrow - the first day of the rest of my life.

Sitting in a full carriage on the train home it was as if there was nobody but me. My mind so preoccupied with what I'd just done. I didn't know how or what or when, but I knew my time was now.

But suddenly doubt creeps in, what on earth am I doing? what will I do for money? The work has stopped but the bills keep coming. I've done my time, I am so fed up of scraping the barrel, counting down to the next pay day, living in overdraft and hoping my card doesn't get declined. The only comfort I have are my Mother's words "Kerry it may be long, but not forever."

It took time but once I had the clarity around what I wanted,

I set out my vision. I started creating Vision Boards in a very specific and purposeful way. I needed the answers to two specific questions:

- What is my life going look like?
- What kind of impact do I want to make on the world?

Thinking aloud I decided to start doing what I always do - helping others. I was good at that. I enjoyed it. I could make a difference.

Next, I looked at how I wanted to show up in the world – what was my mission? I knew it had to be something so much bigger than me – to the point where it seemed impossible to achieve on my own. Then it showed up when I joined The Brand Builders Club and Sammy got me clear on what future I wanted my business, my family and I to have … My mission is to help one million people globally, to stop exchanging time for money. My whole being lit up even though I had no idea how I was going to accomplish it!

I've forgiven myself for those fourteen hideous years. I've learned to care about myself, put myself first and take time for me. Now I'm creating something, my future is no longer scary, it's exciting. I know I have the power to change. There's so much more to me than what the past has shown. Something evolves inside me. I feel like a bird in a cage, but this time the cage door is open. It's up to me to fly free.

As I shared my story with more and more people, things started to change. A whole new business started to emerge. Based on the astounding results of helping others, the You are not your job program was born, guiding changemakers to transition from Employee to Entrepreneurs or to progress if they have already taken the leap. I started to build my brand as The Employment Escape Artist. My goal was to support others to also become free and help them on their entrepreneurial journey, coaching and mentoring them to also share their stories in an engaging, compelling and magnetic way. The more I shared, the more people asked for my help and the more alive I felt at knowing that I could genuinely help them.

Stories are essential to building your brand as an Entrepreneur. They are the quickest way to build rapport and also showcase your expertise. Unfortunately, too many get it wrong! Trust me, there have been many times I have wanted to rescue a Speaker from themselves because their storytelling is so bad!

How Do You Tell A Great Story That People Actually Want To Hear?

So, what is the secret to good storytelling? Firstly, it is absolutely vital that you have a good structure. As someone who now coaches, trains and mentors Entrepreneurs to be world-class speakers, let me share some tips with you:

Well the clue is in the sentence. The fact is that you don't want to be 'telling' a story at all. That's half the problem, and this is where so many people get it wrong. The biggest tip here is that you need to re-live it. A story needs to be re-lived, that's a guaranteed way to breathe life into any story. You need to really go there emotionally before you even open your mouth or start typing. People are not silly, they can get the lessons they need indirectly.

Always Set The Scene...

Setting the scene gives context for your audience. The truth is we all have stories and experiences that have shaped us. But remember that your audience was not there at the time, they don't really know you and you need to let them inside your head, so they can share these intimate experiences with you through your story.

Get to The Problem Early...

In the beginning of your story, get to the problem early. You want to avoid a lengthy introduction because it delays getting to the action. People want you to get to the point, to understand the problem you are trying to solve.

Take Your Audience On A Roller-Coaster...

Roller coaster rides are exciting, sometimes up and sometimes down but never boring. You're either screaming or anticipating. It's exactly the same with your story. Think about the ups and downs you went through. Seldom are problems solved straight away, what new learnings did you discover? At the end let them know how you transformed.

Focus on Your Client or Audience...

Your story is for them... not you. This tip gives the added bonus of taking the pressure off you and helps to reduce anxiety or feeling vulnerable during your story. Be warned vulnerability in your story is very powerful, but don't make it so far-fetched that you become incongruent and miles ahead of your audience, or you run the risk of disconnecting from them. For example, I don't tell the story of when my partner got murdered abroad. Why? Because most people cannot relate to that experience.

Add Some Humour...

This can be done in the most serious and heartfelt stories to give the audience a chance to breathe. Especially if you have a very emotionally charged or academically heavy topic. After intensity it helps to lighten the mood.

Belief...

Another well-known myth people believe is that great story telling is a God given talent that you are born with. Well, I'm here to tell you that's simply not true. Great story telling is a skill, just like any other skill. It can be learned and mastered with great guidance and intensive practice.

Great Storytelling Enhances Your Brand Success...

Clients love a great story. It stands you out from the crowd and businesses like mine are built on the power of knowing how to construct and tell your story. Are you ready to tell your story?

And one last golden nugget before you go... Always have conflict in your story with something or someone. That's where the excitement happens!

Kerry Bartley - The Employment Escape Artist

Kerry Bartley is an award-winning International Public Speaking Mentor, NLP Master Practitioner, CEO of You are Not Your Job.

Headhunted and sought out to deliver training to entrepreneurs globally, Kerry has for the past ten years been the *Secret Weapon* to the world's most eminent Speakers. In 2019, Kerry launched the *You Are NOT Your Job Program* - going from £0 to £10,000 in just three weeks!

In January 2020, Kerry launched her international online communities - *Stand Up, Speak Out* and *You Are NOT Your Job*. Affectionately known as The Employment Escape Artist, the jewel in Kerry's crown is that she is able to shortcut your route to success through her proven expertise and skill.

Whether you crave escape from the trap of full-time employment, or fear being stranded in an uninspiring business, Kerry is proof that change is achievable inside 12 months.

www.youarenotyourjob.org

www.linkedin.com/in/employmentescapeartist

Facebook community: you are not your job

The Art of Conscious Connection...
How To Open Doors
Through The Power Of Laughter

Brigitte Keane - The Laughter Liberator

"You Are Perfect The Way You Are. You Are Unique. The World Needs You. Remember that YOUR Laughter Is Your Super Power."

Did you grow up hearing that 'Laughter is the best medicine'? What happened? Do you feel like you laugh enough now? Why don't we hear about the many benefits of laughter and the laughter lifestyle as we grow up? This is very unfortunate, because I believe that we are all born laughing.

As a new-born baby, the first developmental milestone is when the baby smiles. Smiling continues throughout early childhood, when children laugh up to 400 times a day.

We, as adults however, laugh on average less than ten times a day. What happened to us in between? I believe that laughter was educated out of us. It was considered silly, superficial and inappropriate.

It seems that we have forgotten about the many benefits laughter has for our physical, emotional, spiritual and social wellbeing... from mental stress relief to the physical health benefits and social behaviour that it has a massive impact on. How about happiness, social connection, improved morale, creativity and productivity? Laughter is a universal language of global communication. Laughter connects – no language needed!

In my travels all over the world, I have witnessed first-hand the impact that laughter and the laughter lifestyle is making on lives. I have also experienced the transformational impact that laughter had on my own life. I chose the name, "The Laughter Liberator" deliberately when I joined The Brand Builders Club, because laughter literally liberated me and it can liberate you too.

Laughter affects every area of our life and is our connection to our soul. We all have the ability to laugh, although it might be hidden like a diamond deep inside us – covered with dirt and cobwebs, waiting to be rediscovered. Think of me as your joy partner, guiding you through creative and supportive solutions to reconnect with yourself. I invite you to join me on that journey.

Whilst speaking at a college in India, a professor told me that this was the first time in ten years that he had laughed. Can you imagine? I did not know whether I should be happy or sad for him. No matter where I speak around the world, the situation has always been the same: we do not laugh enough. There was a time when I was guilty of that myself.

Despite laughter always being present as I brought up my three small children, I never really paid attention to the valuable contributions of laughter in our lives. My life was serious and I was a perfectionist. I never felt good enough and suffered low self-esteem, despite my outward success. People saw me as a role model. But inside I was screaming out with fear and frustration, I did not know how I could survive all of the assaults coming at my family and me. I felt like a helpless victim. I wish I had known then what I know now ... that I always have a choice. I am unique and only I can do certain things. I am happy and strong. My life load is much lighter.

You are destined to live a beautiful life, not a miserable one. For this, you have a superpower... laughter! I am asked all the time how I got into the laughter lifestyle. Perhaps this story will tell the tale.

"Pastor, Pastor!" a woman approached me, "My mother is a completely different person now." I asked her to tell me more. She told me about how her mother had joined a laughter club, which met every morning at a local park. "Wow," was my first thought, "How silly is that?" The woman continued, "Do you think we could do something like that at our church?" That day changed my life. Consequently, my congregation had a laughter circle every Sunday after church. The surprise was that the whole congregation participated!

I conducted a laughter session once in Cambodia, to a mostly female audience. The participants were so taken with my presentation that they had a hard time focusing on the next speaker. I literally had to go to the back of the room, out of their sight. We had lunch and still, people were giggling and laughing. This lasted all throughout the afternoon. Laughter even continued on their way home. What an amazing legacy that is!

Let us take a closer look at the health benefits of laughter. Consider our magical, physical body and the many health benefits that laughter offers for our body, which is our temple. Why would people refer to our body as a temple? To me, the body as a temple makes perfect sense, because I believe that divinity is deep within us all, and we are all divine beings. Is it not amazing how our bodies are self-healing, as long as we are feeding them with the right nutrients? The body is a masterpiece, one of the most powerful and intricate systems ever created.

If we compare our body to an automobile, we need to ensure we are using the correct fuel. If we instead fill our tank with bad fuel, or something like milkshakes, the engine will sputter before dying. The engine would be damaged and the car would not start. In comparison, if we fill our bodies with the wrong nutrients, our bodies will continue to work for a while, even while filled with toxins. The body collects the offending toxins and processes them potentially through an illness, while ensuring that we can continue to function. Of course, taking care of our body is of the upmost importance. Laughter and the Laughter Lifestyle make the body happy and nurtures the body in conjunction with its other needs of sleep, rest, relaxation and work.

Why is self-care important? Because it affects our health. Laughter affects our health in a positive way. Our body showers us with feel-good hormones. Endorphins and oxytocin raise our mood, boost our immune system, bring more oxygen to our brain, help our breathing, lower blood pressure and strengthen our immune system.

Did you know that ten minutes of deep belly laughter has the same effect as any other thirty-minute aerobic exercise?

Moreover, that laughter boosts our immunity for up to 24 hours? It is like jogging for our intestines and a massage for our internal organs. Laughter makes us happy and forms connections. Laughter makes us more human and welcoming. Laughter forms community and builds emotional intelligence. It opens doors.

I want to encourage you to use your superpower - laughter, and to live the Laughter Lifestyle from this moment on. Do you know that your body cannot be stressed when you are laughing? Laughter is an immediate stress buster. When your body is stressed, it ceases all nonessential functions. It believes that a tiger is chasing it, and the body uses all available energy to escape this metaphorical tiger. The fight or flight syndrome is activated. Only, there is no tiger. We have learned that 90% of diseases are stress related, and laughter is the antidote to stress.

As we come to a close of this chapter, I want you to remember that laughter is indeed the best medicine and your superpower.

We have the fastest remedy for stress always available. We know that laughter is anti-stress and positively affects our health. Our bodies like laughing and so do other people.

Laughing is fun and contagious. It boosts morale and makes us happier. Why would you withhold such a priceless gift from yourself and others? Why not make the Laughter Lifestyle YOUR lifestyle? Reap the social benefits that laughter offers, along with benefits for your mind, body and spirit. Become a global peacemaker and connector. Sprinkle your life with magic, compassion, gratitude, empathy and love.

I invite you to get started now and join our community in Laughter Lounge Global.

See you there!

Brigitte Keane - The Laughter Liberator

Brigitte Keane is an internationally renowned healer, speaker, author, theologian, educator, consultant and the creative visionary behind her pioneering movement, The Laughter Lifestyle.

She is a creative and inspiring joy partner, who provides her clients with creative and nurturing solutions that enable them to reconnect with themselves to feel joy-ful and happier, releasing the laughter that exists in their soul.

With more than 20 years experience traveling the world as a laughter professional, Brigitte is passionate about sharing the sacred healing power of laughter. Inspired by the life-changing experiences of her own life, Brigitte invites others who are imprisoned by the grind of their daily life to play and experience the liberation of the Laughter Lifestyle.

Brigitte is on a mission to improve the self-esteem, self-confidence and happiness of people all around the world and believes that by supporting each other, the world can become a win-win place.

Brigittekeane@gmail.com

bit.ly/LaughterLoungeGlobal

The Secrets Of Effortless Success...
How To Stand Out, While Fitting In

Ellen Loopstra - The Art-of-Alignment Accelerator

*"Personal Inspiration, Creativity And Talent
Is Where The Real Magic Is In Your Business."*

It may or may not surprise you, but 70% of all professionals worldwide are unhappy in their job! If that figure does surprise you then, congratulations, as you are probably one of the ones who has discovered a career that aligns with your interests and talents!

I believe that everybody, and I really mean everybody, has at least one talent - whether you are aware of it or not! In fact, we are all carrying a whole suitcase full of personal talents around with us - maybe some are yet to be discovered – and those talents, combined with our core-values, and personal life-story makes us a unique human being. Yet so many of us are so absorbed with comparing ourselves with others that it is making us miserable.

It's time find your own personal fulfilment!

'Your time is limited! So, don't waste it living someone else's life!' - my favorite quote by Steve Jobs. It's as if he knew that he was going to die at 56 years of age, and leave the world with a huge legacy. He knew, like I do, that every single day that we struggle to reach success, is one day too many.

I know this because I once experienced the feeling that there might not be a tomorrow, which is why I am so passionate about this. Let's go back to the summer of 1984.

It is a beautiful sunny day at the beginning of July, and there I am sitting at the back of the classroom, by the window, when in he walks with a pile of papers in his hand. Ugh! That teacher has taught us for years and I despise him. He is a piggy-eyed man who often used to humiliate me in front of the class. But this time I am feeling confident. My dear, supportive mum - a tall lady with an open mind and a no-nonsense attitude – had been calculating my average scores at school, and we believed my hard work has paid off, and that I have passed. "Bring it on!" I'm thinking to myself.

The next second, I'm losing it. I feel my eyes drowning with tears; the adrenaline rushes to my head, while I ask him, "A mistake, sir?" The paper he just handed over to me shows me that I haven't passed and that I am not going through to the next grade. "Kein Fehler!" he answers shortly in German, "No mistake!" I am noticing the nasty grin on his face. The next moment I am running for the door, slamming it behind me as hard as I can. I hear my footsteps echoing in the tiled hallway. Doubts were kicking in... again. Maybe they were right about me at primary school? Maybe I AM just a 'dumb blond'? While running, I'm convincing myself never ever to come back again.

Of course, I did return to finish school. In our Dutch culture, not having the certificates to show that you have completed your education, means you are labeled as a "drop-out" for the rest of your life.

So, I graduate after seven years of torturing myself, by studying for hours and hours on end. When I'm telling my Dad that I passed my exams, it took about ten minutes of convincing him before the good news sunk in. My eldest brother, eight years my senior, and who also worked hard told me to double check at school.

Out of all of this disbelief, the worst rumor that I have to face is that I have been labelled "a fraud". My grades were so extraordinary that the teachers don't believe that I have done it all on my own!

Unfortunately, this lack of encouragement did not stop there.

During my entire school career, from primary school to university, I was discouraged over and over again from choosing options based on what I liked or what I was good at. However, by working myself to the bone and conforming to the rigid rules of the various school systems, I achieved the dream I had at primary school - to be a "graduate" at university. From then on I could call myself a Physical Geographer, specialised in landscape transformations.

Now I certainly proved that I was not stupid at all!

But those doubts were still there, long into my working career. Rather than following my gut feeling, I kept trying to meet the expectations of others. I was stifled, and I was losing myself more and more.

Until that one morning I am woken from a very deep sleep by a friendly voice from above whispering, "That was a close call. It would be wise, not to do that again." It was the Intensive Care-specialist. Oh no, not another baby lost... again?

Four years ago I had lost my other baby while working in a corporate culture that did not fit me at all. My 'manager' seemed to rule over my team AND my life. They had the nerve to fire me after just three weeks recovery, having given birth halfway through my pregnancy and they told me to *Recover, and wait until we have a solution.*

After this, the cantonal court sent me the official papers.

A friend and highly experienced cantonal judge did advise me to use my energy for my recovery, because this company wasn't worth fighting for.

And while I'm receiving my next shot of morphine, I solemnly promise myself that once I am recovered that I would use MY creativity, live up to MY talents, MY values, MY BEING, and find companies and systems that I personally and professionally select myself.

And I did... successfully.

Here are a couple of things that I learned during all of those years that you can take away right now and implement yourself...

You Are Sitting On A Ton Of Value...

You are definitely sitting on a ton of undiscovered value if you don't know what your talents are. Like I mentioned earlier, you are probably carrying a whole suitcase full of talents. Tapping into those talents makes life so much easier. Living your life using your talents in alignment with your professional purpose will get you in flow effortlessly. If you don't you will lose track of your own values, your inspiration and creativity. You might experience your work as being really hard, resulting in working even harder and longer trying to make THE difference with your contribution to society. Working that hard, you run the risk of becoming overwhelmed, frustrated, exhausted, ill, easily distracted or burned out. You may find yourself making poor critical decisions in a state of stress. You are literally killing yourself, your private life, professional life and even your business in the end. The magic begins the moment you decide to be yourself.

So find out what your talents are to start living in alignment with your talents and feel the flow.

How To Stand Out...

While discovering your talents, you might 'bump into' your values. Having those two figured out, you are not done yet. To be effortlessly successful you have to look really closely at your life-story to reveal your everlasting drive. What is in there that the world needs and what you can provide just by being you. Your talents, values and drive will reveal your professional purpose. I encourage all professionals to select a job or build a business in alignment to their personal story... or at least a part of it. Only then you will totally embrace on all levels the one thing you stand for, enabling you to STAND OUT, positioning yourself to change and influence the world on a small or global scale.

Find out your purpose in life and define your desired contribution to the world you're in, based on who you truly are.

Don't Fight To Fit In...

Have you ever felt you tried so hard to follow the rules and procedures you were faced with, but did not succeed in fitting in the system or the society you are in? Not even when you are giving all you've got working as hard as you can. Working yourself into the grave is not the solution. A bad system will beat every good person anyway. No matter how talented that person is. Be aware of the fact that NO is a strong answer! NO stands for 'NEXT OPPORTUNITY'. A 'no' will guide you towards your next move into the right direction more effectively than you can imagine.

So you better pay attention when you witness one door closed, because ten others are opening at that moment.

Realign If You Have To...

Dare to be creative and authentic. Find your authentic way to fit in and contribute in a meaningful way doing your job while building your career as an employee or manager or building and growing your business as an entrepreneur. Find your own creative way to connect within the systems of society to have an impact on many people making THE difference. Alignment is key. Realign if you have to. If you live your life in alignment it feels like you never have to work again.

This is the biggest Secret of Effortless Success.

Could you visualize yourself constantly contributing in a meaningful way - based on who you truly are? Is that what you think your effortless success might look like? Now is the time to overcome your mis-alignments, finding your personal fulfilment and be effortlessly successful every day. I'm rooting for you all the way.

So, are you ready to Stand Out, while Fitting In?

Ellen Loopstra - The Art-of-Alignment Accelerator

Ellen is an Inspirational Change Leader, Transformational Business Mentor, International Speaker, Leadership Coach, Trainer, Teacher and CEO of the AlchemICT Alignment Academy.

As 'The Art-of-Alignment Accelerator' she is passionate about mentoring individuals, teams and organizations on *How To Stand Out, While Fitting In* to be effortlessly successful.

Ellen has experienced what 'being out of alignment' feels like: a constant battle to adapt, and to fit into the educational systems or organizational structures and procedures that don't fit your personality. She lost track of her personal self after being determined to 'fit in' and meet society's expectations. She noticed that other professionals were doing the same, holding up a professional facade and not fulfilling their potential.

This led her to start her own business and develop the *AlchemICT Alignment Approach,* to boost businesses and their leaders by aligning personal talents to their professional missions, thereby bringing out the best in both. Her systemic, simple strategy with a touch of artistry enables her to mentor the clients she works with to boost their success almost instantly. Something most people take a lifetime to achieve. Are you ready to Stand Out, while Fitting In? Stop struggling and start being effortlessly successful from today!

http://www.alchemict-alignment-academy.com/Membership

https://www.linkedin.com/groups/8916062

Mind The Gap...
How To Stand Clear Of The Noise

Martin Ramsden - The Business Kickstart Mentor

"If your eyes have been opened to what you must do, then do it. Failure to act is commercial suicide."

If you think about the business journey you set out to achieve, are you on course and on time? If so, well done! Of course, most business owners start with ambitions of a higher purpose or a dream. But after as little as three years, many lose sight of what that dream or purpose was and lose their way. If you are not on the right track or moving close enough to achieve your dream, you have a GAP.

MIND THE GAP - you need to resolve this. So I will share with you how you can change this situation. How you can focus, gain clarity and understand what steps to take, to achieve your higher purpose or dream.

If you are serious about achieving what you set out for you and your business, do not leave this to chance. Hoping things will improve can produce the opposite result. So, unless you have a genie in a lamp with wishing credits, do not wait even one day longer! This will worsen your frustration and increase your anxiety.

You and your business serve a purpose. Your customers buy

from you and want to buy even more from you. But if your business is not effective, your customers will suffer too. You owe it to yourself, and your customers to get on with this starting today.

I have mentored many people to deal with this situation, but I never dreamed that I would have to resolve a serious gap of my own.

I started a company with a plan to help aspiring consultants from their job to independent freedom. By mentoring them to help other business owners, I would accelerate my mission. I want to support over one million business owners, and I know that by making small changes in their businesses this can lead to great results.

I did this with a business colleague I had known for seven years. We had a great relationship and shared the same dream. The business was great, we were recruiting and training experienced business developers. We were gaining contracts to support companies in several countries. We had an identity that inspired both consultants and clients who viewed it as a global brand.

I had ignored considerable back pain for too long though. I dreaded the months of recovery after surgery. I put it off until my consultant neurosurgeon told me that I risked nerve damage unless I had the surgery. So I discussed the situation with my business partner who agreed it was not a problem. With phones, email, and internet we had the means to work anywhere.

The surgery to rebuild the base of my spine was a success. But during ten days in the hospital, I could not get hold of my partner. Instead of looking forward to getting back to work, life took a different turn.

A web developer I didn't know called me to ask for my website login. I thought that very strange so enquired further. It turns out that my partner asked him to change my company address and contact details! I still could not get hold of him. What was going on? The following day I received court proceedings from two of the consultants. They were seeking to recover their training costs. They too were unable to get hold of him.

When I finally tracked him down, I discovered he had moved ALL OF the sales revenue and contracts to a different company while I was having a life altering operation. He told me that I was no longer involved! He failed to steal my company, my website and my intellectual property, but he did succeed in stealing the business, leaving me with all the debts.

What would you have done? My first thoughts were anger and frustration! These soon passed as I had to focus. I had lost 18 months of momentum, I had lost a lot of money, and I had lost the business. This created a bit of a gap!

I decided to treat myself as a client and do a gap analysis. The difference between my situation at that time, and where I wanted to be. I looked at the numbers, and what I would need to make up ground and time. I also looked at how I could use my Strengths to:

- Overcome my Weaknesses

- Maximise any Opportunities, and

- Minimise future Threats.

Maybe you recognize this as what most marketers call SWOT; I did two of these. The first on my current situation, and the second thinking ahead (where I wanted to be).

I have been doing this with clients for years. But it takes courage and honesty with yourself to stand back and take a satellite view of your own business. It is even harder to dig deeper and be objective about the issues. My entrepreneurial wife kept me in check!

How do you know if you have a gap? In simple terms, this is by comparing where you are now, with where you want to be in achieving your dream or higher purpose. But what exactly is going on, and what do you need to fix? You will need an effective plan and know how you can measure the criteria which will drive your success. This is the process I have used with clients (including myself!) time and time again.

Tip! Look out for Cause and Effect. Are you looking at the effect of something else that is the cause? This can trip you up.

Step 1 - Analyse Your Current Situation.

Be thorough! Otherwise, you will be depriving yourself and those you hope to serve.

- Identify your strengths, weaknesses, opportunities, and threats (this will be SWOT 1).

- How will you measure each of these points? You can measure them by a monetary value, such as 'I want to earn £10,000 per month, but where I am currently is £1000 per month'. Or you can measure it by numeric values, such as 'I want 100 customers, but where I am currently is 12 customers. In either case you can see the gap clearly by knowing where you are and where you want to be. Otherwise, use a consistent method to rank them (from 1 to 10).

- No guessing or assumptions are allowed here!

Step 2 – Think About Your Ideal Situation.

Be creative and visualise what the future looks like.

- What is the date?

- What does success or achievement look like? Step into it, picture it, feel it, live it.

- What metrics or ranking have you achieved so that you know you have arrived?

- Now determine your future strengths, weaknesses, opportunities, and threats (SWOT 2).

Determine what your future strengths must be for you to achieve your goals. Weaknesses must improve, but remember perfection is unlikely! Better opportunities will doubtless come your way in your new successful situation. Assumptions about future threats are allowed. For example, technology and economic changes. You will revisit this several times.

Step 3 – Mind The Gap (But Look Into It)!

Now you can uncover what is missing!

- Compare SWOTs 1 and 2.

- Check that you will have massive progress.

- If you do not see a massive difference, go back to Step 1 and start again.

- Now test the difference between Strengths 1 vs Strengths 2, Weaknesses 1 vs Weaknesses 2, Opportunities 1 vs Opportunities 2, and Threats 1 vs Threats 2.

Step 4 – Bridge the Gap!

From your Step 3 evaluation, what actions must you take?

- Set goals with timescales. Be realistic.

- What steps must you take to achieve these?

- Set aside time without distraction in your calendar.

- Revisit the whole process as you move forward.

- Commit.

- Get help if you need it (mentoring, coaching, team, outsource, etc).

The Business Tools

For clarity and focus, SWOT is a way of zooming in on the things that matter.

- Strengths and weaknesses are internal to your business.

- Opportunities and threats are external (you cannot control these).

- Think of as many points as you can.

- Use your team or people who know you and your business.

It is important when brainstorming points NOT to discuss their validity as it slows down or stops your thinking and momentum. Don't judge what comes up. Keep your energy high and only list them. Once you have the list, that is the time to qualify them (what does each point mean)? If necessary, you can group any in the same category (e.g. Strengths) that express the exact same thing.

If you work for your customers and forget to work on your own business and personal development, your business is at serious risk. You need to get comfortable with using simple techniques that will help, and set aside some quality time on a consistent basis to measure where you are in comparison to where you want to be.

The most successful companies do this on a weekly basis.

Just Do It

Some people reading the actions above may be inclined to put this off as being hard work. People have a habit of procrastinating. It is human nature to put off doing something we do not want to do. But you (yes YOU!) are different. You now know that if you are stuck and not on track to reach your dream or higher purpose, you have a GAP. It will not close itself. It will get bigger and eventually consume both you and your business. You know you must act and acting now will create a lot less work than acting later to undo something that has already been done.

You owe it to yourself and your loved ones. You also owe it to your customers old and new, who want you to be successful. You can do this even if you can only find 15 minutes a day or an hour a week. Just make sure there are no distractions.

If your eyes have been opened to what you must do, then do it. Failure to act is commercial suicide.

You can do this!

Martin Ramsden - The Business Kickstart Mentor

Martin is a High-Performance Business Coach and Mentor, International Speaker and Creator of *The Frustration to Freedom Blueprint;* a 12-month program that supports entrepreneurs and small business owners to attract more customers, keep more customers and make more profit.

His passion is inspiring and supporting business owners to optimize their personal, team and company performance developed from techniques utilized with over 5,500 leaders from many different business disciplines, across many cultures in over 34 countries.

In 2002 he gained accreditation to provide much-needed help for Small to Medium Size Enterprises and became a lecturer at a residential business school for new coaches and consultants. He was a founding coach of the Executive Coach Business Development Program and is now on a mission to support over one million business owners to make the small changes in their business that will lead to big results.

www.MartinRamsden.com/loba

https://www.linkedin.com/in/martinramsden

Building The Strength Of Your Brand... Through The Calm Of Your Mind

Alice Law - The Calm Creator

"A calm mind is our greatest strength, but a calm soul is a weapon against anything."

As I sat beside my beloved Dad at dinner, talking to him with the hope of trying to ignite a conversation, my heart sank when I realised tonight would be yet another night when the stress on his mind and the depression in his energy had taken over his desire to participate.

I sighed wondering if I would ever again get to see the engaging and charismatic man I had grown up with. The answer sadly was no.

The events in his final years had been heart-breaking for our whole family, but it was stress, the unspoken killer, that stole him from us in the end. Taking him not once, but twice - first mentally, then physically.

I realised that despite his age, we could have had him with us for so much longer and to me, as a daughter who truly adored her Dad, it was devastating.

After he died, I made a promise to myself that I would help end this mental pandemic. I wouldn't let it keep devastating other families and I would never let it take me over as well.

We live in a time where being 'stressed' has become the new normal. We constantly hear people around us say how 'busy' and 'stressed' they are, like it is a trophy - but the underlying reality is that stress is the silent killer.

Stress is the killer of our relationships, of our productivity (by 31%), of our ability to deal with problems effectively. It kills romance, our energy, our happiness and eventually even our physical selves. With sick days from stress related illness rising every year and the stressors in our lives not going away, there has never been a more imperative time to take our mental fitness, and the ability to manage and prevent stress more seriously.

Growing up, stress was never really a part of my life. I had a fortunate upbringing, with wonderful parents who loved us, a great education and amazing experiences. My Dad was a successful entrepreneur, but he always knew the importance of making time for his family and I really admired him for that. Overall, bar his brief brush with cancer when I was just three, we had a tranquil and easy life.

Little did I know that would all change.

Stress can be caused by many different outside factors: health, family, finances, work, home and romance. Outside events happen and they affect us. What I wasn't prepared for, was for them to happen all at once.

My eldest and half-sister Suzanne was suddenly diagnosed with cancer in my final year of university. We were shocked and worried, but she was a true fighter and we thought she had won her battle with it, until suddenly it took over her completely, and nearly four years later, it took her from us. This naturally devastated our family, but my Dad in particular struggled greatly with losing his eldest child – having lost his own twin to cancer at the same age. It was an echo of the worst of his past repeating itself and this time with his own child – every parent's definitive nightmare.

After the global financial crisis of 2008 caused devastation to so many businesses, deals that my Dad was expecting to happen started to unravel and he found he was suddenly having to worry about his businesses, his family's financial future and his daughter's health all at the same time. It took its toll. He laughed less, drank more and had an aura of distraction and worry around him.

After Suzanne died, things seemed to go from awful to worse. We were forced to sell our family home and my Dad had to deal with not just his grief, but also the stress of an unprecedented legal battle with people he had thought to be true friends, financial uncertainty and the loss of his home. Everything he had worked so hard to build slowly evaporated before him. It was too much for him to bear and he was taken over by stress that rolled into depression.

Depression consumed him and started to affect his health, slowing his body down. Having furthermore been rushed to hospital just two days after my sister's funeral with a blood clot, the doctors also found he had tumours in both his lung and pancreas. I fought hard with him over his health for the next few months, desperate not to lose another family member and adamant that he needed to get answers as soon as possible, but he had given up. He had no intention of going through any gruelling treatment again - to him denial was the simpler option.

As time passed I watched my Dad become more and more consumed by the stress of trying to salvage the last of business, of financial worry and the heartache of grief - and the charismatic, self-assured, mischievous and inspiring person I had grown up with slowly disappeared in front of my eyes. It was heart breaking to watch, and I missed him greatly, feeling like I had already lost the Dad I once knew.

Helplessly I watched him suffer in both mind and body, until we lost him irreversibly and suddenly to a large stomach ulcer that caused internal complications.

I was worried about the cancer taking over one day, but in the end, it was the silent killer stress that won.

I dealt with these events alongside my own struggles of heartbreak, and later redundancy, and I came to the realisation that if I didn't learn how to deal with stress in a different way then it would also consume me. I had already felt its sting on my own health in the form of IBS, which led to my own cancer scare. I knew that something had to change. If everything around me was out of my control, then that something that I could control, had to be me. So, I learned and absorbed as much as I possibly could, discovering a new way of thinking, being and coping.

That new way of living is what has protected me, after Dad was gone, the stark reality sank in that the effects of stress were what took him from us in the end. Learning to not only manage it, but to prevent it taking hold in the future, is what has protected me through it all.

I have come to know that preventing it as much as possible, and managing it as best as possible, is a two-part process – one of calming and getting to know your mind, and of connecting and understanding your soul.

You can have as calm a mind as you like, but if your soul is stressed because you are not living true to your own values, integrity and purpose, then you will struggle to find true inner calm, because you will be going against what your very core is guiding you to. Just as you can have a connection and intuitive dialogue with your soul, but if you can't quiet your mind or you don't know yourself inside out and what triggers your negative thought patterns, then you will let that voice take over and always make poor decisions based on stress and fear.

Learning how to calm your mind and tap into the natural calmness of your soul is arguably the greatest strength there is. It will prime you to being the calm and charismatic leader of all of aspects of your life - professional and personal.

Learning to access this calmness on both a logical and spiritual basis, comes from what I have named *Triple PI– Perspective, Presence, Purpose and Intuition.*

- If you can master your mind by really getting to know it, you will be able to shift your perspective, not just on the outside stressor itself, but in your own response to it.

- If you can log into presence as much as possible, living in that space between reaction and response, you will be engaged in the life around you and better able to choose how you respond to stress, instead of reacting in the moment.

- If you can connect to your core identity and understand what soul purpose you are here to live out, you will live it whilst living true to your values.

- If you can learn the difference between the voice in your head and the voice in your heart, the guidance of your gut and the voice of your intuition will move you in the right direction.

Being conscious of these four things will give you the key to calmness – and you will be able to unlock and rely on that strength whenever you need and most importantly, choose to.

Calmness is a skill in itself, if it wasn't then the whole world would be calm. But I also believe it's our forgotten natural skill, that we need only to relearn.

Great decisions, creativity and connection are all born from a space of calm serenity. They are the choices, ideas and relationships we make and build that last, as they come from an unwavering knowing within. When you let the outside stressors in your life and the built up thoughts of stress in your mind, and tensions in your body take over, then you have not only put your health and happiness at risk, but also your ability to execute with excellence in the professional and personal decisions that matter most.

Decide now whether you want to be the calm and charismatic leader of your life and business, or if you will succumb to a mediocre version of yourself, reacting continuously under stress. Calmness is the definitive skill that will help you to make a large and truly sustainable impact in the world around you, bringing out the very best of yourself and your efforts.

Outside stress will always keep appearing, that's simply life - but it's up to you to decide how you want to answer to it.

Alice Law - The Calm Creator

Alice is a Stress Management and Holistic Performance Coach, 5-Star Rated Podcaster, International Speaker, Reiki and Intuitive Expert and Founder of Lawali Life.

As *The Calm Creator,* she teaches leaders & corporations how to strip away stress and guide them back to balance, so they can be the calm, charismatic and successful leader in all areas of their life and work.

Alice understands stress from a unique position after she went through chronic stress for a seven year period, personally experiencing the truly damaging effects of it when she experienced loss in every aspect of her life at once.

From this experience she discovered her most effective process to not just manage stress but to prevent it going forward. Having lost her own father to stress related illness, it is now her mission to help as many people as possible to dis-identify from stress and live in their natural state of calm.

www.lawali-life.com

https://www.instagram.com/lawali_life

https://podcasts.apple.com/za/podcast/lawali-life-podcast-with-alice-law/id1496364101

Social Media Matters...
How You Do Social Media
Is How You Do Everything

Carole Fossey - The Social Media Mentor

*"Social Media is not something you DO,
it is a channel to reflect who you ARE."*

Do you spend hours on social media and suddenly realise the morning has disappeared? Perhaps you have been "doing" social media but struggling to make it work? Maybe you see others 'crushing it' on social and wonder where you are going wrong. Well, if that sounds like you, you're in the right place!

But first, let me take you back to October 1996 – before Social Media was a twinkle in anyone's eye. I was working at an IT recruitment company. I was hired because I was a great salesperson and internal recruiter, but I knew nothing about IT. So, I was given 12 months back copies of Computer Weekly to read.

I noticed this thing called the internet kept cropping up... at first just one article every couple of editions, then weekly, then several articles weekly. It was clear that the authors of Computer Weekly believed the internet was the next big thing, as did I.

I asked my boss if she would pay for a 2-day internet course

I'd found. Her response was, "The Internet? No-one has that, it'll never take off". She clearly hadn't been reading Computer Weekly!

So, I took two days holiday and paid for the course myself. And that began my lifelong love of tech, the internet, and all things digital.

When LinkedIn came along in 2003 I was straight on it – and was later surprised to get an email in 2013, from the founder thanking me for being one of the first few thousand people on the platform.

And I soon saw the application of social media for my business at the time – recruitment. When I sold the recruitment business in 2014, I knew exactly what business I was going to start next and Strategy Social Media was born.

So, what makes the real difference in a successful social media strategy? Take it as read that you know your customer inside out and know exactly what they need (huge subjects for another day).

The key is to understand what it is that will make people choose YOUR (fill in your own products or services here) over your competition.

And it is here that you find the answer to all your social media questions.

Because, you see, most people start in the wrong place when thinking about social media. They are wondering how they can use it to sell themselves, how they can benefit from it. And, of course, we all want that. But it is the wrong question.

The right question is what are my values and therefore the values of my business? What are you doing it all for?

You might answer that you are doing it to make money. But that's not it. Very few people are motivated by the money – it's what the money represents that really motivates them.

Why did you start your business? Was it to be able to control your own destiny, so that you could choose to attend your child's school play or drive your son 20 minutes to college every day to save him an hour and a half commute (or is that just me?!).

If you do one thing today, sit down quietly for a few minutes and go back to why you wanted to start your business, or why you want to start one now, and identify your core values.

Core values are the ones you cannot live without.

Mine are Family, Fun, Learning, Teaching, Innovation/ Creativity and Kindness.

I started my very first business back in 2001, and those values applied then and now. I have to learn – it's not that I like to – I HAVE to! Learning new things drives me on and stops me getting bored. That's one big reason why I started a social media business – because things change on a daily basis. And I love keeping up to date with everything so I can teach my clients – (another of my values – sharing knowledge).

When you know what your values are – it makes it easy to make decisions in your business. In fact, it makes ALL the decisions in your business easy. Do I hire this person/do this kind of marketing/develop this new product? Yes - if they match your values.

And so, what you do on social media must reflect your brand values.

If your values are to help – then THAT is what your social media must do. If your values are to have FUN – then your social media should be fun.

Knowing who your customer is and what they want, will help you develop messages that appeal to them – it will get you in front of your ideal client. But you are not the ONLY one in front of them. The sales will come from people resonating not only with the message but with your values – as expressed through your brand.

For example – here's a topical tweet I saw from Old Spice on April 27th (2020), *You can't social distance from your nose!*

Some people will find that hilarious, some will raise a wry smile, and some will think it insensitive. That doesn't matter, what does matter is their audience likes it.

Fun and humour are definitely part of their brand values and are therefore reflected in their social media which – you will notice – is not trying to sell anything.

Remember people go to social media to be social. They go for a bit of EIEIO. Which means they want to be:-

- Educated – they want to learn how to do something – cut their child's hair, rewire a plug.

- Inspired – they want to be taken out of themselves by inspirational quotes or stories.

- Entertained – people want to laugh or watch things that make them feel good.

- Informed – this is a big one – people are looking for news. People want to be the first to know something so they can break it to their friends.

- Offer - occasionally coming across a no brainer Offer might pattern interrupt them – but it has to be truly valuable and something they are interested in.

Most social media is "top of funnel"– people don't know who you are, they don't care about you at all, they just want EIEIO. At this level, it HAS to be about a combination of what they want and your brand values.

If your brand messaging resonates with them – then you can look at strategies to take them further down the funnel – for example into a Facebook group.

In a group, the focus should still be on delivering what they want to see, in a way that is congruent with your brand values. And here is where they can get to know, like and trust you, and eventually you become the brand that is first in their mind when they want your product or service.

If you are in a position to spend money on advertising then do it. But don't make the mistake of thinking ads are all you should be doing. That's the, *Where's the money?* thinking, that will not build relationships.

Some people may buy directly from ads – but most people won't and so it is all about building relationships. If your page or your group has no posts, your adverts won't work. Your audience and Facebook will see that you are just in it for the sale and will frankly, be turned off by that.

Let me give you the example of Sophie who works in social care and runs a part time photography business. She's a great photographer, but to you and I, looked like any other photographer in terms of her website, branding and offering. We worked with Sophie to identify her brand values, and from that she realised that Fun, Innovation and Family Communications were key.

She developed a way of combining her passion for helping families communicate and for photography into a new service – Quirkography. Family Fun Days with beautiful and unique photos at the end.

But you can't just sell that service to people who don't know you. It's about building relationships. So here is what we helped Sophie to do. She created Free Family Activities To Do At Home – a Facebook group that already has 528 members as of today. And a low priced Quirkography 'Family Fun Pack', that she is offering through Facebook ads.

The brand fills a need – what to do with the kids at the weekends. But it goes further than that. It resonates with parents who want to form deeper connections and better communication with their kids while having fun. In other words, it resonates with parents with the same values as Sophies.

They can see that she is living her values, she is therefore also being of value to her target audience and she is growing a huge community, who one day might need a family photographer. And who are they going to think of when they do?

That's the way to do it!

So, remember - how you do social media, is how you do everything!

Carole Fossey - The Social Media Mentor

Carole Fossey, The Social Media Mentor, is an award-winning coach, author and TEDx speaker. She is also the Founder of Leading Women in Business and the Get Sh*t Done retreats, where she coaches and supports female business owners to cut through the complexity of marketing and social media, to focus their attention on getting their brand out into the world.

Carole was non exec Director of the largest Chamber of Commerce in the UK, Greater Manchester (GMCC), (2003-2016). She was particularly focused on small female led businesses, leading the Chambers women in business group and writing for their magazine, which is where she decided to commit her time to helping those female entrepreneurs thrive and have more fun.

Today Carole and her team coach and support businesses to discover and live their values, and communicate those values through the smart use of social media to attract their perfect clients.

Website Strategy Social Media www.strategysocialmedia.co.uk

Twitter @CaroleFossey https://twitter.com/carolefossey

Instagram @carolefossey https://instagram.com/carolefossey

Pinterest The Social Media Mentor https://www.pinterest.com/ carolefossey

Facebook Carole Fossey https://www.facebook.com/carole.fossey

LinkedIn Carole Fossey https://www.linkedin.com/in/ howtointerview

A Case For Congruence... A Path To Creating Clarity, Confidence And Connection

Vicki Ibaugh - The Course Creation Coach

"When you walk your talk, people start to follow."

For 30 years I was the ideal employee. I was a people pleaser, a loyal and committed worker, and a bit of a perfectionist. I took what I was asked to do and did it very well, leading to hundreds of courses and substantial profits for my employers. I was the *go-to, get it done, and make it look great* employee. I never missed deadlines, even if it meant early mornings and late nights.

Then it all changed.

So, did I just quit being the *ideal* employee after 30 years?

In a way, I did. It started with a series of events, but the key incident was a single phone call. It was a simple request from my boss asking, "Can you work today? We have projects due and clients are calling." So why would such a request be so upsetting? Why would this call change everything?

Well, let me share where I was when that seemingly innocuous call came. I was in the pediatric intensive care unit sitting with my only child, my 11-year-old son, whose head was covered in bandages with multiple wires coming out. Just a couple days earlier surgeons had opened his skull up to place more than

100 electrodes on the surface of his brain. All so they could figure out what part of his brain to remove to stop the seizures that were robbing him of his childhood.

Clearly, work was my last concern. It was that moment and the callous intrusion of a request to work that made me realize I could no longer be the ideal employee. My boss had not even taken a moment to ask about my son. It was clear my work life was no longer congruent with the rest of my life. In fact, it had not been for quite some time. While being the *good* employee, my health suffered, my relationship with my husband was strained, and my own spark of creative passion was nearly extinguished. My work was slowly killing me. It just took this perfect storm to make it crystal clear that I could no longer continue on this path. Something had to change, and fast!

This was my wakeup call. It was the flashing sign announcing that I was not living a congruent life. So, what does that mean? What exactly is congruence? At its most basic level congruence is harmony and compatibility. If you apply that definition, it is clear my work was not in harmony or compatible with my personal life.

As with many changes, the first step is to become aware there is a problem. I was now acutely aware there was a problem. What was not clear was what to do about it. That leads to the next part of the process: *Getting Clear.*

Before I could be congruent, I needed to first get clear about what mattered most. Some key questions I asked myself during this time: *What do I value?* and *What are my biggest priorities?*

Once I got clear on my values and priorities, I was able to apply the test of congruence by asking: *When I look at my life and my average day, am I living my values and priorities?* In other words, am I walking my talk? If I say family is my highest priority, are they a key part of my day or relegated to whatever time might be left when the work is done??

Keep in mind my congruence and yours will look different

depending on our personal values and priorities. That is the great thing about this process. You get to choose what is important to you and honor that.

In my case, when I looked at my day, I was not congruent. My family was not coming first, and there was no time in my schedule to focus on my health. Now that I was clear on what mattered, I started scheduling my priorities first and then fit other people's priorities around the time left. This was my first step to becoming congruent, and it also led me to quit my job so I could honor the value of family more fully.

So, what does my personal congruence have to do with Brand Attraction? For me, it was the first step toward creating a business that worked with my life instead of being my life. My experience has been that as entrepreneurs our personal values and priorities often overlap with our businesses.

By starting with my own personal clarity and congruence, I found that I was able to create the same for my course creation business with greater ease.

In fact I began with those same questions of, *What are the values and priorities of my business?*, and then expanded into *Who do I want to work with, what services do I want to provide, and what does that look like?* I assembled all the pieces and parts essential to developing a clear brand.

Just as in my personal life, I needed to test if what I said was important passed the congruence test. The question I asked was slightly different, but at the core the same: *When I look at how I run my business, am I being congruent with the values, mission, and vision of my business?*

For example, if I say I provide high-level coaching, do I really do that? If I say I value integrity, do I operate my business in an honest manner? If I say I value impact, do I create impact for my clients? When you can answer 'yes' to these questions, it not only checks the box for congruence, it increases your internal confidence that you are delivering on your promises.

Another wonderful thing happens from this congruence. Your clients become clear and confident on what to expect from you and your business. If your client's order is correct and on time every month, they are going to be confident you can be trusted. If you say you treat clients like family and you call to check up on them after an appointment, they indeed feel like family. When you are congruent, your client feels confident and trusts in your business. Those two things are like gold for any business.

Lose them and your business and brand will suffer.

Congruence can also impact confidence in a different way. Confidence can erode when we provide a service to others that is inconsistent with our personal life. For example, if you are a money coach, but your own finances are a mess and you are on the verge of bankruptcy, you are not congruent. You are not walking your talk. While you may think you are able to hide your incongruence, more than likely it is affecting your personal confidence and your ability to attract and keep customers. The best way to fix this problem is to take action to get congruent in your personal life. In this case, repair your finances and get back on track. Once you do, your confidence will return and create an attraction factor. You can even use your own story of success to increase your credibility.

Another way congruence can improve your business (and life) is when it is used to support you in making clear decisions. The question I ask is this: *Is doing (fill in the blank) congruent?* For example: Is attending the local after hours open house event in congruence with my personal and business priorities? For me saying 'no' is a common response to evening events, because this is my family time. You can see how congruence becomes the measuring stick for even the smallest decisions. It becomes your secret clarity tool for when to say 'yes' and when to say 'no.'

The final bonus of being congruent is connection. As I became very congruent with how I ran my business and how I lived my life, I began to connect more and more with my ideal client.

It was as if by being in harmony with my values I became a magnet for people who shared similar values and who were looking for the services I provided. But also, by being congruent, my trust and confidence increased and my business grew. I guess I should not be so surprised. When we see others like us, we create a connection and from that we begin to build trust based on seeing consistent congruence in how they behave and conduct business.

Today, I look back and realize that phone call was actually a gift. It was the gift of leading me to congruence, of restoring my health and family, and of creating a business that has enabled me to create an impact I never would have had if I had continued to be the *ideal* employee.

So, I leave you with this question to ponder: How are you being called to be more congruent, and what impact might that have on your own life and business?

Vicki Ibaugh - The Course Creation Coach

Vicki is a certified International Speaker, Best-selling Author, Documentary Star, and founder of The Course Creation Studio; where entrepreneurs learn how to translate their knowledge into courses that create impact and get results.

After more than 20 years of instructional design experience and building hundreds of courses for hospital systems, the Centers for Disease Control, and the U.S. Department of Defense, she decided that it was time to make a bigger impact and have more time for her family.

Today she coaches and teaches entrepreneurs how to harness their knowledge superpowers to create "get-results" courses that transform the lives of their clients, transforming their lives and businesses in the process.

www.TheCourseCreationStudio.com

Control Your Leads Or Someone Else Will... How to Put Your Business on Thrive Drive

Sarah Cox - The Funnel Builder

"Creating a profitable business that works on auto-pilot is easy when you know how!"

If I asked you, *"What is the biggest problem in your business right now?"* what would you say?

You'd probably say something similar to me when I was first asked this question.

It could be that it's hard work. It relies on you. If you're not working, you're not earning. You don't have enough enquiries. You aren't fully booked. There's too much admin. You need help, but you can't afford it. It is eating into family time.

It's very common to feel this way – it's not always as easy to set up a business as you initially think it will be.

There are two common things that small business owners want, which normally relate to the reason you originally set up your business:

TIME and MONEY.

Time to spend with your family or friends. Time to do something you enjoy.

Money so you don't have to worry about a pension, can afford to do and buy what you want, and provide for your family.

Everyone has their own reasons for wanting more time and money, but ultimately it's about the freedom to do what you want, whenever you want without having to worry where the money will come from to do it.

In a traditional job, you work for an hour and get paid for an hour.

As a small business owner, it's often the same plus you usually end up doing unpaid work to get your business up and running and working even harder than you did in your 'job'.

Business owners often think that if they create a great product or service, they will make money from it.

But business isn't just about providing a great product or service. Business is also about getting your message out to people, being good at marketing and selling your product or service to people who need it.

How do we get out of this trap of trading time for money and create a business that makes money and time for us?

The answer is by having AUTOMATED MARKETING SYSTEMS. This is the key to getting more enquiries, more customers, more income and more time.

Before I talk more about this, I want to share a bit about my business growth journey...

I haven't always done what I do now. I followed the traditional path of school, university, job and had a corporate career in Human Resources.

After 19 years, I didn't want to be in an office, working long hours every day for someone else and doing the same thing for the rest of my working life.

As I drove to work, I used to see people in the park and in cafes and wondered what they did that meant they weren't travelling to work like me.

I realised I didn't have the freedom to do what I wanted every day.

I decided I didn't want to wait until retirement to do what I wanted.

I dreamt of doing my own thing; being my own boss; working when I wanted to; enjoying what I was doing every day; getting fitter and healthier.

So, in 2012, I decided to set up my own business as a Pilates Teacher.

This was all very exciting and I couldn't wait to get started BUT...

...I didn't know ANYTHING about building a business, how to tell people what I was doing or how to find clients.

Hence, my journey into the world of online marketing began. I learned many valuable strategies, which I applied to my Pilates business, enabling it to grow to 20 classes a week.

During this time, I discovered that my true passion was for online marketing. I set up another business to help entrepreneurs grow their business using automated systems.

I found there is ONE thing that most small business owners struggle with the most. Any ideas what it might be?

Well, if I tell you what mine was when I started teaching Pilates, you might agree that it's the same for you.

Without doubt my biggest struggle was getting enough customers.

I tried using leaflets, adverts, business cards, social media and joint ventures and all bore fruit; just not enough quickly enough.

So, I found a business mentor and followed some successful entrepreneurs. And do you know what I found?

They all have one KEY thing in common.

They find leads and turn them into customers and then into repeat customers on autopilot.

How do they do it? Well, I call it *The Simple 5 Step Formula To Turn Leads Into Sales.*

These are the five steps that I discovered:

1. Audience

One of the key questions for any business owner is: *Do people know about you?*

You can have the best product or service in the world, but it's no good if no-one knows about it. The more people who know about you, the higher the number of customers you have.

You need a group of people who want what you've got to fix the problem they've got.

2. Attract

How many people know about you, but you don't know them? How many people would be interested in what you offer if they knew you existed?

These people could become your customers and you're potentially losing them right now to someone else!

You need to attract potential customers to you and get their contact details when they find you.

Building a database of people who are interested in your products and services, so you can then "talk" to them is critical to success.

3. Acquire

Next, you want them to become a customer.

Now that's not necessarily easy, as they've only just met you. They may need some convincing that what you've got will help them BEFORE they buy from you.

You need to engage with your leads and build a relationship with them through an automated process to convert them into buying customers.

4. Amount

How much are your various products and services? How much money does a customer spend with you on their first and subsequent purchases?

Once you know this, you can work out how many customers you need to enable you to achieve your financial goals.

5. Attachment

How often do your customers buy from you? The more often they buy from you, the better for your business and bottom line!

You want your customers to become 'attached' to you and become a fan of yours, so they want everything you offer.

You want them to buy something else at a higher value or to make a regular purchase, such as a monthly subscription.

Think about how much easier it would be for you, if you have something people want to buy again and again and are pay-ing for it automatically, without you having to chase them for payments.

So, that's an introduction to *The Simple 5 Step Formula To Turn Leads Into Sales.*

Now, I'm guessing you might be thinking, *It all makes sense and I can see why I need the 5 steps in place in my business, but where do I start?*

Firstly, focus on automating the process of getting more people aware of you and then capturing the contact details of people who find you. This enables you to take control of your leads. It enables you to communicate with them about who you are, what you do, their problems and how you can help solve them.

Not all your leads will be ready to buy when you are ready to sell. Therefore, you need to be in the forefront of their minds when they are ready to buy. Otherwise, they will look for someone else to provide the solution to their problems and you've lost your leads to someone else.

That's the worst outcome for you – they found you first, they now want what you do, and they go to someone else...

You want to avoid that happening to you!

Instead, imagine waking up in the morning to find you have new people in your database and that some of those people have bought your products or services, all whilst you were asleep.

How much better would that be?

If you haven't got a way to attract your ideal client to you and collect their contact details using an automated system and process, NOW is the time to put this in place.

Don't let people who would be an ideal client for you and you an ideal solution for them, go to someone else who might not have as good a product or service as you, but is better at sales and marketing than you.

By implementing *The Simple 5 Step Formula To Turn Leads Into Sales* in your business, you too can have a thriving business that brings in leads and turns them into customers on autopilot.

To book a complimentary Lead Capture Consultation with me to find out how to set up automated marketing systems in your business to enable you to live the life you really want, go to:

https://sarahcox.clickfunnels.com/consultation

Sarah Cox - The Funnel Builder

Sarah is an International Speaker, Marketing Funnels Coach, Consultant and Founder of The Funnel Builders Club.

Having spent 19 years in Human Resources in the corporate world, Sarah launched her own business Nutripilates in 2012, a nutrition and Pilates business, as she wanted to focus on her own health and fitness as well as help others. Sarah had to set up a business from scratch, find clients online and automatically take bookings. She discovered a passion for being an entrepreneur and for marketing automation.

In 2014, Sarah pivoted her business to become a full time Marketing Automation Expert. She now supports entrepreneurs with getting more leads and turning those leads into customers through automated systems to increase their income and free up their time.

Sarah works with entrepreneurs worldwide to build their landing pages, sales funnels and email marketing campaigns, enabling them to focus on serving their clients. She believes that there is no better time than now to start automating the marketing of your business to get more enquiries, more customers, more income and more free time.

sarah@sarahcoxmarketing.com

www.sarahcoxmarketing.com

https://www.facebook.com/groups/sarahcoxmarketing

https://www.linkedin.com/in/sarahcox2

https://twitter.com/sarah_cox

https://www.instagram.com/sarahcox.marketing

How to Transform Your Vision Into A Global Movement

Marie Diamond, Global Transformational Speaker, International Best Selling Author And Master Teacher In The Secret

"Visualise your dreams daily and manifest your goals every minute of your life."

How do you take your vision and transform it into a global movement? If you have seen or read *The Secret* the #1 Global phenomenon of the personal development industry, you will have watched something that became a global movement and reached more than 500 million people all over the world. As a result of being part of the movie and the book, my message has reached all of those millions of lives. But how did it come about and how did I become part of this Law of Attraction movement and become one of the top Speakers in that field.

Let me take you back to when I was just fifteen years old. I was at high school in Belgium, where I grew up in a lovely part of the world called Bruges. This day was like any other school day; only it ended with a twist. A truck almost killed me in an accident, and I had what is referred to as a Near Death Experience. I went to 'the other side'. It was filled with pure, bright light and I heard a voice that told me it was not my time to die. I had to go back because I hadn't yet fulfilled my purpose. I asked what my purpose was, and the voice said, "To enlighten more than five hundred million people."

I had no idea what was going on or what any of that meant. I thought Enlightenment must mean 'making a difference in the world'. I took my purpose very seriously and started taking my first steps to manifest this right away.

I started by asking daily requests. I use the term God, however you could use the word Universe, Source or something else that you want to call it instead. In the morning I would say, "God, I am here to enlighten more than five hundred million people. Please show me how." While waiting for the answer I decided to start making a difference wherever I went. I would smile at everyone I saw. I was very badly bullied at school, so I would even try to be nice to my bullies. I was making a difference in every small way I could, but I knew that to make a bigger difference I would need to step up my game.

I calculated that if I could make a difference to just one person every day, then by the time I was 80, I would have enlightened around 23,360 people. If I lived to 90 that would be 27,010 people and it was starting to add up. But I was really struggling to see how I was going to get to over five hundred million.

I started visualising and connecting to what you call the law of attraction. Although I was just a teenager, I had already met my Spiritual teacher when I was just seven. So, I had been meditating secretly since that young age and knew how to practice the art of visualisation. I loved drawing so I started drawing pictures filled with people from different cultures all around the globe. Every day I was connecting to these people through my meditations and telling them to "join my purpose". At that time, I didn't know how it worked, I just had faith that it would. I also added the Law of Attraction into my environment and set up my bedroom in such a way that it reflected my purpose. I started using the Feng Shui principles that lead me later to become the #1 Western Feng Shui Master with millions of students all over the world.

Out of High School, I set out to find a profession that would help me to achieve my purpose. I thought, 'If I become a Lawyer, I could start working for the United Nations or become a Minister in Belgium. That will help me to reach millions of people.' So, I studied Law and became an international lawyer, working for the Belgian and European government. I was moving forward in reaching millions of people. After all, I was working with top political leaders and working with Supreme Court Judges and the Ministers of Justice.

I really felt like I was making a difference, but not in the way I really felt was enlightening. At 31 years old, I started a consulting company where I was consulting, coaching and teaching people about Meditation, Feng Shui and Enlightenment. I knew a lot of 'alternative information' as people now call it, but I'd been doing this a long time before I realised I could build a business doing it! I put the word out to see what would come of it.

My first private clients were actually politicians I had worked with before. They were impressed with my style of working with them. They asked me about how I was manifesting everything I wanted so easily and always without stress? They asked me how to be more joyful and how to feel better? I had not foreseen that they would ask questions like this! But I started answering their questions and teaching them everything I knew. I was going into their offices to work on the energy of their workspace using Feng Shui. I was coaching more and more people and I was even being asked to start speaking about it to larger groups. Now I was an executive spiritual coach, a motivational speaker and teaching Meditation and Feng Shui Seminars.

Before I knew it, I was asked to speak internationally at seminars and conferences in European countries, which was definitely helping me to reach more people. But I needed to start running my own seminars and workshops if I was going to reach 500 million people.

I remember the first time I set up my own motivational seminar. I sent invitation flyers to 40 people and wrote, 'I'm holding a seminar where we will meditate together and I will share how you can make a big difference in your life.' Out of all those people, not one person showed up. Not even my mother, my husband, or my friends. And I thought, 'Well, I can just pack my things and leave. Or I can give my speech for two hours and imagine that 500 million people are waiting on the stairs!'

I stayed and delivered that seminar and I visualized that in my chairs millions of people were listening.

Within six months I had 3,000 people attending my seminars, talking about meditation and spirituality. I knew that for every day I was visualising my vision, I was building more and more attraction.

After a few years, I got a download in one of my meditations that I needed to visit California and start speaking there about my work. I didn't even know there was a whole industry that was already building around motivation and spirituality. To the North of San Francisco, I set up an event and booked a room with big windows. I didn't know why at the time, but yet again nobody had shown up. I again imagined that the room was packed and started to speak to the chairs as if each seat had thousands of people sitting on it. Before I knew it, in that hour and a half, 15 people walked into the room because they saw me speaking from the street – through those big windows! And one of those people said, "I want you to come and speak at my place next week" and so it developed into bigger audiences.

After going back and forth from Belgium to America, one morning I woke up and this voice in my head shared another message, "Marie, you have to move in three weeks". I caught myself saying out aloud, "We've only just bought a beautiful Villa. I just put all my savings into it. How can we move now?" I told my husband that we have to move in three weeks and that he had to start packing. He just stared at me. "But we've got this huge house and a mortgage, Marie" he said. But he also knew that he had married a woman with a mission.

So, I arrived in America in just three weeks with only a few suitcases. I had literally $2,000 and the rest of all my savings were in the house we'd just bought. There I was in a new country with a small number of students and a visa that would last me for three months to work. I rented a house in California for a year, even though I knew I could only be there for three months. I took a leap of faith. And when I arrived, my students had gone into their garages and had furnished my entire house with the things they no longer needed. I will never forget that day, expecting to walk into a house with nothing in it other than my suitcases. As a surprise, they turned that house into a home for me, knowing that I needed to set to work on achieving my 500 million mission as soon as I landed.

Within two weeks, I was doing a workshop in the San Francisco Bay Area. I knew I needed 30 people in the room, or I would not have enough money to live for the next month. Only 15 people had booked onto it, but again I had faith. One person arrived in the morning and told me, "There are more friends coming, but it will take them a few hours to get here." By 12 o'clock the last person that showed up was the person that would transform my Life: International best selling Author, Marci Shimoff. She became my client, my student and my friend. Within a month, the word had spread as Marci started telling everyone about me. Before I knew it, I was speaking at big seminars and events in California and was working with John Gray, Jack Canfield, Bob Proctor, Marianne Williamson and many other Transformational Leaders and Celebrities. They were looking for a spiritual mentor and Energy Master because they were hitting a glass ceiling with their work and they needed to up their Law of Attraction.

One day I created a new vision board and put a little yellow Post It note on it that said, 'I am going to be in a movie seen by millions of people that will transform the World.' So, I bought an Oscar and put my name on it! Now within a month, I had my first Oscar winning client calling me out of the blue. "I've heard about you and want you to come to my house because we're stuck", said the voice on the other end of the phone. My career just kept moving forward, because I was just doing everyday whatever I could do to make a bigger impact and to manifest my purpose. Now I have more than 20 Oscar winning clients in my portfolio.

Visualising the millions of people that I am here to enlighten stayed my daily practice, even in California. Then, I became pregnant with my youngest child. My daughter used to speak to me through my dreams and she told me that she wanted to be born in Santa Barbara. Now, at that point I was in the Bay Area, so I started going back and forth to Santa Barbara to find the house she had shown me in the dream.

While I was consulting for Jack Canfield's home in Santa Barbara, I found the house, just one mile away from his estate! As soon as the family and I moved into that house, my entire life shifted to a whole other level. One day Jack said to me, "I have this gathering in my living room, where I bring speakers and authors in from all over the World to get together that are the top leaders in the field of Transformation". Then he said, "Oh, and by the way, I need somebody from Europe and you're the only one I know!" I hesitated and told him I am not one of the top leaders. He said to me, "Marie, one day you'll be as famous as everybody that I've invited". I accepted the invitation that would transform my journey to reach millions.

At that meeting, I walked into this room that was filled with all these amazing speakers and authors who have sold millions of books and had millions of followers and students. Even though I had achieved so much already, I still felt so small in this room full of giants and really considered what I was even doing in that room. I sat myself at the back, feeling like a fish out of water.

I sat next a guy who turned out to be the CEO of Learning Strategies, the #2 Home study company worldwide. Within six months, they produced my Diamond Feng Shui home study course that sold to more than half a million people over the last 15 years. Saying yes to Jack Canfield created another huge opportunity to me.

In our third meeting of the Transformational Leadership Council at Jack's house, I met another person that would become the source of me achieving my 500 million mission. A blonde woman with long hair from Australia called Rhonda Byrne came to sit next to me. She told me that she was doing a movie called 'The Secret' for a TV channel in Australia and asked if I wanted to be interviewed. This was my first TV interview ever and I thought, "Well if I can enlighten millions of people in Australia, that's fine by me'. Many big names in the motivational industry said no to her interview and I am sure they regret it profoundly now!

When the movie came out and it became a Global hit, many of my much more famous colleagues asked me, "Marie, why are you in this movie? You were so unknown". My answer to them was "I have been visualizing since I was 15 years old that I am here to enlighten more than 500 million people. It was on my vision board to be in such a movie that would transform millions of lives. Was it on your vision board?"

What lessons can you learn from this story of a lifetime? Here are five things I did to achieve my mission and continue to make a Global impact that you can take from this book right now and start doing too…

Step 1

I ended up in the movie 'The Secret' by visualizing it. When you see it clearly in your mind, the universe sets to work on setting it all up for you. But then you have to set to work on Step 2 right away…

Step 2

I took inspired action to achieve it. You can visualise all you want, but if you don't take action to take what you saw in your mind out of your mind and make it happen in reality, you will not get the results you truly want.

Step 3

I took my knowledge of Feng Shui for Success and Abundance into every home and office that I have lived and worked in. If you don't have a success corner where you work that is in your field of vision every day, set to work straight away on setting up your success corner. You can work out the best place for your success corner by downloading my Marie Diamond App at http://mariediamond.com/apps

Step 4

Create a big vision that requires you to step up and step out from comfort and mediocrity. Ask the Universe every day in your prayers and meditations to show you the opportunities and to meet all the people that will help you to manifest your big vision. If you find it challenging to meditate, you can listen to my guided meditation called 'Tubes of Light', also on the Marie Diamond App.

Step 5

When these people show up, say YES to them, even if you feel still too small or not ready. When opportunities and people show up, it is because you are totally ready to take your business and brand to a new level of Success. The universe will never put in front of you that which you are not ready for.

So my friend, I wish you all the happiness, abundance and success in the world. Now it is up to you to go and make it happen.

Best wishes,

Marie

Marie Diamond, Global Transformational Speaker, International Best Selling Author And Master Teacher In The Secret

Marie Diamond is a globally renowned Transformational Teacher, Leader, Speaker and International Best-Selling Author, Creator of Diamond Feng Shui, Diamond Dowsing and the Inner Diamond Meditation Programs. She is also the only European star in the worldwide phenomenon "The Secret".

She is a global household name in the field of Energy, Quantum physics, the Law of Attraction, and ancient Wisdom like Meditation, Feng Shui and Dowsing to support individuals, organizations and corporations to transform their success, financial situation, relationships, motivation and inspiration.

She is a founding member of the only Global Transformational Leadership council, Founder and President of the Association of Transformational Leaders of Europe and is considered as one of the 100 Transformational Trainers, Speakers and Authors in the World.

Recognized as a Global Energy master, she is known for her love of people and her ability to explain very complicated spiritual and energy knowledge in a practical and down to earth way. She is a successful spiritual businesswoman that loves being a mom of 3 children and enjoying her journey with her husband of 30 years.

For more information on how to create Magical Living, visit Marie at *www.MarieDiamond.com* and follow her on Instagram at: MarieDiamond8

How To Be In Our Next Book

Join us in the next Law of Brand Attraction book to share your business growth story and inspirational message with the world.

Please email *sammy@howtobuildabrand.org* with your 150-word biography and a short (no more than 250-word) overview of the story and key message you would like to share.

Sammy will then get in touch with you to share how you can get involved.

One thing is for sure though... if you've got an inspirational story that you believe will support other business owners to make more impact and income doing what they love, we want to hear it!

How Do I Find Out More About Brand Builders Club?

The Brand Builders Club is an invitation only membership, where each and every member is invited to join personally by Sammy Blindell, the Founder.

To build a relationship with Sammy, join her free group on Facebook and start showing up!

Join here: *www.facebook.com/groups/howtobuildabrand*